"Stories are transform
transformation. The ˢ
a journey through Jeˢ
with timeless stories ᴛ
commentary and practical reflections make this book an essential companion for anyone seeking to align their life with the wisdom of Jesus's parables. This book is a journey toward intentional living and spiritual growth and highly recommended for anyone desiring a deeper understanding of Christian faith and practice."

—PAGE BROOKS
Missional Lead of Missio Mosaic Society
State Command Chaplain (COL) of Louisiana Army National Guard

"You hold in your hands an invitation into the storying world of Jesus that has all the potential to transform you and your world. Andrew Ray Williams, as a faithful guide, knows how to welcome us as readers into these stories—stories to transform us for the Kingdom. Read on and be made new."

—RICK WADHOLM JR.
Associate Professor of Old Testament at
Assemblies of God Theological Seminary

"Andrew Ray Williams has masterfully connected the parables of Jesus with modern-day applications. By opening up about his own life with vulnerability, he weaves a tapestry of stories that builds trust and inspires faith. His inclusion of thoughtful questions for personal reflection and small-group discussion challenges each reader to apply the lessons of Jesus's stories to their daily lives."

—DURANT KREIDER
Associate Supervisor for the Atlantic District of Foursquare Churches

"Storytelling has always had a powerful role in the formation of culture and faith. Andrew Ray Williams's *The Stories That Make Us* invites us, his readers, to revisit the familiar texts of Jesus's parables as a means of reigniting, reinvigorating, and reorienting our lives to the principles of the kingdom of God in practical and profound ways. In this timely work, Williams's pastoral heart, scholarship, and invitation to reflection provide a fresh take on the biblical stories that shape who we are and who we are becoming. I highly recommend it!"

—JENNIFER THIGPENN
Multiethnic Ministry Coordinator, The Foursquare Church
Associate Pastor, Pasadena Foursquare Church

"Andrew has masterfully and beautifully brought the parables of Jesus to life in our modern context. As I read, I felt like I was sitting in a comfy chair with a cup of coffee across from a wise pastor as he shared how to walk in the love and grace of God. This book takes the profound truths of Jesus's parables and makes them accessible and applicable to any follower or seeker of Jesus. A great discipleship companion for a new believer and a needed refresher for us 'seasoned' believers."

—MARK CHESTER
Lead Pastor of Gettysburg Foursquare Church

"With the deep pastoral insight of Andrew Williams, the ancient parables of Jesus inform contemporary stories that guide our steps in a troubled world. Through the Spirit who is always present, the common occurrences of life become opportunities to discover the ways and works of God in our lives. These messages encourage and strengthen the soul. They inspire us to walk in faith."

—DAN TOMBERLIN
Assistant Professor of Pastoral Ministries at
Pentecostal Theological Seminary in Cleveland, Tennessee

"In *The Stories that Make Us*, Andrew Ray Williams brings the parables of Jesus to life. Drawing on his rich experience in preaching, he seamlessly weaves these ancient stories into the tapestry of contemporary life. This book transcends the conventional reading experience, offering a journey that connects deep spiritual truths to everyday realities. Whether you are a devout follower or just exploring the teachings of Jesus, you will find Andrew's insightful narrative both enlightening and transformative. I wholeheartedly recommend this book to anyone seeking a deeper understanding of the parables and their impact on daily living."

—RYAN LYTTON
Assistant Professor and Director of Academic Services at Life Pacific University-Virginia

THE STORIES THAT MAKE US

THE STORIES THAT MAKE US

Practicing the Parables of Jesus

Andrew Ray Williams

The Stories That Make Us
Practicing the Parables of Jesus

© 2024 Andrew Ray Williams
All rights reserved.

This material may not be reproduced in any form, published, reprinted, recorded, performed, broadcast, rewritten, or redistributed without the explicit permission of Andrew Ray Williams. All such actions are prohibited by law.

Hardcover: 979-8-9906278-0-2
Paperback: 979-8-9906278-1-9
E-book: 979-8-9906278-2-6

Library of Congress Control Number: 2024940296

Author photo by Millpond Photography

Unless otherwise indicated, the scripture quotations contained herein are from the New Revised Standard Version Bible, copyright © 1989, Division of Christian Education of the National Council of the Churches of Christ in the U.S.A., and are used by permission. All rights reserved.

Scripture quotations marked NIV are taken from the Holy Bible, New International Version®, NIV®. Copyright © 1973, 1978, 1984, 2011 by Biblica, Inc.™ Used by permission of Zondervan. All rights reserved worldwide. www.zondervan.com. The "NIV" and "New International Version" are trademarks registered in the United States Patent and Trademark Office by Biblica, Inc.™

Scripture quotations marked NLT are taken from the Holy Bible, New Living Translation, copyright © 1996, 2004, 2015 by Tyndale House Foundation. Used by permission of Tyndale House Publishers, Carol Stream, Illinois 60188. All rights reserved.

Scripture quotations marked MSG are taken from *The Message*, copyright © 1993, 2002, 2018 by Eugene H. Peterson. Used by permission of NavPress. All rights reserved. Represented by Tyndale House Publishers.

Published by
Hillside Publishing
P. O. Box 907
Fishersville, Virginia 22939
hillside-publishing.com

To Brandon Williams, a fellow preacher

In the end, we'll all become stories.
—Margaret Atwood

Tell all the Truth but tell it slant.
—Emily Dickinson

The Kingdom of Heaven is like...
—Jesus of Nazareth

CONTENTS

Foreword by Andrew Arndt 1

Preface 5

1
The Parables of Gates, Sheep, Trees, and Foundations 10
Standing and Falling 13

2
The Parable of the Wheat and the Weeds 26
Growing Together 29

3
The Parable of the Unmerciful Servant 44
Forgiven but Unforgiving 47

4
The Parable of the Wedding Banquet 62
Wedding Clothes 65

5
The Parable of the Ten Bridesmaids 82
Keeping Watch 85

6
The Parable of the Three Servants 100
Stewarding Our Views of God 103

Postscript 121

Works Cited 122

FOREWORD

O*nce upon a time,* a prophet said to a king, *there was in a certain town a poor man with few possessions who owned a little lamb. It ate and drank with him and his children at his table and even slept in his arms. It was like a daughter to him.*

In that same town, there was a rich man who owned large numbers of sheep and cattle. When a visitor came to the rich man, the rich man took the lamb from the poor man, slaughtered it, and served it to his visitor to eat.

Upon hearing this, the king burned with rage, declaring in his anger that the rich man must die. *You are the man,* said the prophet. And with that, the thunderstruck king crumbled, and the words of Psalm 51 fell from his lips like an avalanche of contrition—words that have now graced the lips of penitents for generations, pointing the way home. "Have mercy on me, O God" (Psalm 51:1).

This story I'm sure you recognize. It is the story of the prophet Nathan's confrontation of King David over the sordid and ugly Bathsheba affair (2 Samuel 12). And in form if not in content, it is the central method by which the Word arrives at the threshold of our lives. "Once upon a time" is the sound of knuckles rapping at the door.

It is worth wondering—what might have happened if Nathan had taken a different tack, confronting the wayward king not with "Once upon a time" but with a moral harangue?

Quite probably he would not have survived the encounter, and King David, beloved of the Lord and chosen to be the first in a dynasty that would culminate in the Messiah, would have lived and finally died in estrangement from the Lord who loved and called him. And what might have become then of sacred history?

We shudder to think about it. And of course, we cannot know. But of this we can be sure: so much depends upon the stories we tell.

What is it about stories? Why do they seem to be much more persuasive than, for instance, data, argument, or sheer proposition? C. S. Lewis remarked that the power of stories lies in their ability to "steal past the watchful dragons of the heart." What a line. We live guarded lives—all of us do—ever watchful against anything like a direct attack on our most cherished beliefs and deeply held values.

And then "Once upon a time" comes along—an unassuming stranger rapping at the door. Our defenses begin to drop as we welcome our guest, whose winsome presence and easy way with words loosens our minds and dilates our hearts.

Ask yourself: how many times have you sat reading a novel or watching a movie and suddenly found yourself pricked in the conscience, sobbing uncontrollably, or gobsmacked by joy? A "mere" story becomes an apocalypse—an unveiling of some mystery of your existence, a key unlocking a door in your mind, a throwing open of the shutters of your heart to let in the clean, pure air of laughter. That's what stories do. Perhaps it is worth saying: no stories are "mere."

Which I think is why Jesus's preferred method of teaching was the use of stories—parables, to be exact. Mark says that Jesus said nothing to the crowds without using a parable (Mark 4:34). And no wonder, since He, according to our creeds and canons, is none other than the "Word" of the One who begins His advent in our lives with a story: "In the beginning God created" (Genesis 1:1). That is to say, "Once upon a time . . ."

Is the whole Bible a parable?

The word *parable*, of course, comes from the Greek. It's a compound word. A verb—*ballo*—which means "to throw." And a preposition—*para*—which means "down" or "alongside." A *parable*, then, is a story "thrown down" alongside our lives, challenging our taken-for-granted view of reality with a God's-eye view. As we toggle back and forth between Jesus's rhetorical throwdowns and our lives, somehow we come to realize that Jesus's stories are not merely nice tales to consider but in fact disclosures of the real environment in which we live and move and have our being. That is, the environment of God's kingdom. Jesus's stories show us where we really are, who we really are, and what is really going on.

A sower went out to sow his seed . . .
There was a man who had two sons . . .
Once there was a landowner who planted a vineyard . . .

Linger with the stories, and they'll do something to you. They'll get under your skin. Provoke and irritate you in all the right ways. Shape and sharpen a fresh imagination for God and His kingdom. Let the reader understand: the important thing is not figuring them out. The important thing is letting them figure *you* out, letting them talk to you. Or better: letting Jesus figure you out by them, letting Him talk to you by them, since they are, in the end, words of the Word who has come to give us life and that more abundantly (John 10:10). You just have to get them in your head, in your heart. As Robert Farrar

Capon has said,

> His parables are not so much word-pictures about assorted external subjects as they are icons of himself. . . . They remain, first and foremost, his way of getting to us. . . . We commit [parables] to the Christian memory because that's the way Jesus seems to want the inside of his believers' heads decorated. . . . Orthodoxy, if it's understood correctly, is simply the constant displaying of the entire collection.

I've been a believer all my life, and I can attest: Jesus keeps getting at me by His stories. Infinitely fascinating, endlessly suggestive, they have been His preferred means for leading me from death to life.

In that spirit, I'm grateful for this volume by the Rev. Dr. Andrew Williams—a primer on a few of the central parables of Jesus. Without explaining them away, as so many treatments of the parables do, Williams sets them before us and opens the door, inviting us to take our first, feeble steps into the country of the kingdom—that is how things are now that Jesus, the Father's "Once upon a time" in flesh, has been raised and enthroned as Lord of all.

I commend *The Stories That Make Us* to you in the words of the Word Himself:

"Listen!" (Mark 4:3).

—ANDREW ARNDT
Pastor of New Life East and Author of
Streams in the Wasteland: Finding Spiritual Renewal with the Desert Fathers and Mothers

PREFACE

In the hustle and bustle of daily life, it's all too easy to slip into autopilot, navigating our routines without a moment's pause to question the direction in which we're heading.

Days blend into weeks and weeks into months, months into years, leaving us hardly a moment to contemplate whether we're living our lives purposefully. It often takes a significant event to shake us from this stupor—a tragedy, like a death in the family, a personal health crisis, or the loss of a job. Such moments, though painful, carry with them the silver lining of reflection, urging us to take a closer look at the lives we are living. It is often in these times of upheaval that we find the precious opportunity to reassess our lives, to ask the hard questions about who we are and what we truly value.

In the first century, Jesus compelled people to confront these very questions. Through His teachings and parables, He jolted those around Him into rethinking their priorities, their relationships, and their understanding of their place in the world. Jesus's presence and message offered a radical reorientation of life's goals—inviting a move from autopilot to intentional living.

The parables of Jesus are more than historical religious teachings; they are vibrant, living stories that resonate across time and culture, holding the power to re-story our lives around what is most true and meaningful. These stories, with their simplicity *and* depth, invite us into a reflective process, urging us to consider not just the narrative of our lives but the values, decisions, and beliefs that shape our existence.

Today, Jesus's message retains its transformative power. When we allow His teachings to penetrate our hearts and minds, we too can experience the jolt needed to escape the monotony of going through the motions. By embracing the wisdom of His parables, we open ourselves to a reevaluation of how we live, paving the way for a life reoriented toward lasting purpose.

My journey into the depths of Jesus's parables began with a realization: often, these stories are either skimmed over with little thought or bypassed entirely. Yet within them lies a wealth of wisdom that demands our attention and contemplation.

Recognizing the need for fresh exploration, I began a preaching series at my church—Church on the Hill in Fishersville, Virginia—focusing on six of Jesus's parables from the Gospel of Matthew. The goal was to highlight the transformative power of these stories for my congregation. The overwhelmingly positive response led me to adapt and expand these sermons into the book you hold today, aiming to reach a broader audience with reworked content that dives even deeper into the essence of these stories that make us.

During the writing process, the insightful commentaries on Matthew by Peter Leithart, as well as Anna Case-Winter's and Stanley Hauerwas's reflections, provided essential guidance. Their perspectives on the Gospel of Matthew helped influence how I interpreted and conveyed the parables of Jesus.

In addition, I have relied on numerous sources in crafting these meditations, yet I chose not to interrupt the reader with footnotes. Instead, I have included a works cited section at the end of the book to acknowledge the sources utilized. I also recognize that certain thinkers have influenced me profoundly; at times, their ideas flow through my writing so seamlessly that I may inadvertently fail to credit them.

This book is structured into six chapters, each centered around a specific parable from the Gospel of Matthew. Designed to challenge, motivate, and transform, these chapters are invitations to see our lives through the prism of Jesus's stories. At the end of each chapter, questions for discussion and reflection are provided to encourage a deeper engagement with the text and its application to our personal narratives. These prompts invite readers to ponder how these ancient stories echo in our current realities and struggles.

In the introduction to his *Forty-Four Sermons,* John Wesley states that his sermons are intended as "plain truth for plain people." He aimed to steer clear of philosophical speculations, complex arguments, and any appearance of scholarly display. Nevertheless, Wesley admits that he might occasionally lapse into these complexities unintentionally. Similarly, I hope that this collection of sermons, now presented as a book, embodies the "plain truth for plain people."

My ultimate hope is that *The Stories That Make Us* will serve as a companion on your spiritual journey, offering insights that provoke thought and inspire change. It is my desire that you are not only able to have a greater understanding of these ancient texts but also a renewed vision for your life, one that is deeply rooted in the truths that Jesus reveals to us through His keen storytelling.

I must express my deepest gratitude to my wife, Anna, whose unwavering support has been a constant source of strength throughout my writing journey. To my church, Church on the Hill: thank you for your encouragement and for being the first to hear these chapters in oral form. Your support has been invaluable. Lastly, I extend a heartfelt thank you to Dara Powers Parker, my editor, whose tireless efforts and incredible skill have profoundly shaped this book. Without her, it simply would not be the same.

The Parables of Gates, Sheep, Trees, and Foundations

Matthew 7:13–28

"Enter through the narrow gate; for the gate is wide and the road is easy that leads to destruction, and there are many who take it. For the gate is narrow and the road is hard that leads to life, and there are few who find it.

"Beware of false prophets, who come to you in sheep's clothing but inwardly are ravenous wolves. You will know them by their fruits. Are grapes gathered from thorns, or figs from thistles? In the same way, every good tree bears good fruit, but the bad tree bears bad fruit. A good tree cannot bear bad fruit, nor can a bad tree bear good fruit. Every tree that does not bear good fruit is cut down and thrown into the fire. Thus you will know them by their fruits.

"Not everyone who says to me, 'Lord, Lord,' will enter the kingdom of heaven, but only the one who does the will of my Father in heaven. On that day many will say to me, 'Lord, Lord, did we not prophesy in your name, and cast out demons in your name, and do many deeds of power in your name?' Then I will declare to them, 'I never knew you; go away from me, you evildoers.'

"Everyone then who hears these words of mine and acts on them will be like a wise man who built his house on rock. The rain fell, the floods came, and the winds blew and beat on that house, but it did not fall, because it had been founded on rock. And everyone who hears these words of mine and does not act on them will be like a foolish man who built his house on sand. The rain fell, and the floods came, and the winds blew and beat against that house, and it fell—and great was its fall!"

Now when Jesus had finished saying these things, the crowds were astounded at his teaching, for he taught them as one having authority, and not as their scribes.

THE STORIES THAT MAKE US

1

STANDING AND FALLING

Two friends were flying from Indianapolis to Muncie, Indiana, on an ordinary Wednesday afternoon in June to have lunch. Wesley Sickle, fifty-two years old, was piloting the small Cessna, while his eighty-one-year-old friend, Robert Kupferschmid, occupied the passenger seat. In the middle of the flight, Wesley suddenly released his grip on the flight stick, flailed his arms, and collapsed. Immediately, Robert, who had never flown a day in his life, took control of the plane, said a prayer, and radioed for help.

Mike Bowen, a pilot of fifteen years, was flying his Cherokee Piper about twenty miles away, doing aerial surveys of gas lines, when he heard and responded to Robert's call. According to Mike's charts, the closest place for Robert to land was Mount Comfort Airport, a public facility with two landing strips just east of Indianapolis. So Mike gave Robert detailed instructions over the radio on climbing, steering, and descending.

In the meantime, emergency crews gathered at the little airport to prepare for a crash landing. Instead of a crash, however, the Cessna hit the runway and bounced a few times, eventually ending up in the soft ground beside the runway with only a bent propeller. Miraculously, Robert was not hurt, thanks to Mike's detailed instructions. In the end, an eighty-one-year-old man with no flying experience successfully landed a single-engine, two-seat aircraft by himself and walked away unscathed.

Without Mike's help, this ending could have turned out a lot differently. But Robert was more than pleased to follow Mike's instructions as if his life depended on it—*because it did.*

Our lives completely depend on how faithfully we are following Jesus's commands.

In Matthew 7, Jesus is wrapping up the greatest sermon ever told—the Sermon on the Mount, which spans chapters 5, 6, and 7. Like Mike's voice on the radio, telling Robert how to safely land his plane, Jesus gives several illustrations in the conclusion of His message that convey the dire importance of hearing and obeying His instructions. It demonstrates something true about the Christian life, though we may not realize it at first: our lives completely depend on how faithfully we are following Jesus's commands.

First, Jesus uses the image of gates to contrast between two ways of being in the world (vv. 13–14):

> Enter through the narrow gate, for the gate is wide and the road is easy that leads to destruction, and there are many who take it. For the gate is narrow and the road is hard that leads to life, and there are few who find it.

Life presents us with different ways of living in this world. Every day we make choices that determine what kind of path we end up on and what future we end up in. And though we might think there are many different paths and many possible futures, Jesus tells us that in the end, there are *only* two: one path to death and one path to life.

It was the same for Robert in the Cessna. He could choose to 1) listen to Mike, the experienced pilot, and probably land the plane or 2) ignore Mike and probably crash. One option gave him life and the other option, death.

Jesus compares the path of life to walking through a narrow gate and the path of death to walking through a wide gate. Both lead to opposite ends. Here, Jesus is echoing the Old Testament prophet Jeremiah (21:8): "Thus says the LORD: See, I am setting before you the way of life and the way of death."

In the history of biblical interpretation is a long tradition of understanding the difference between the two gates as behavioral, as though the distinction is between sinful and virtuous conduct. In that sense, this parable is taken to suggest that there are two choices set before us: to be an immoral person or to be a moral person.

But this interpretation is far too simplistic. Jesus seems to be making a different point altogether.

Throughout His sermon, Jesus discusses righteousness, which is abiding by a divine or moral law, and thus being free from sin. But Jesus describes a kind of righteousness that surpasses that of the scribes and Pharisees, who spent all of their waking hours sticking to the rules (and making sure others did too). Oddly, Jesus says that the scribes and Pharisees are not righteous *enough.*

His hearers would surely have been scandalized by such a notion, considering that these religious elites' devotion to keeping the Jewish Law was well-near perfect. But Jesus knows what He is doing; He is shocking His hearers into understanding that they—along with us—have often misunderstood what true righteousness is all about.

Jesus tells His listeners that righteous *external* behavior doesn't always equal righteous *inward* character. The Pharisees, for instance, obeyed the Law externally, but internally they were filled with rage, jealousy, hatred, and dishonesty. In using the image of gates, Jesus is pointing to the fact that true righteousness is found through a narrower passage—that of the heart.

The pilot Mike Bowen said that Robert sounded "concerned" but never "frantic." I'm certain that Robert felt afraid in his grave situation, and yet he didn't panic. He trusted Mike to see him safely through. But what if he had been so fearful and distrusting that it had affected his ability to follow Mike's directions? Then Robert's inner emotions may have sabotaged his control of the airplane. This is the point that Jesus is making about true righteousness. It's about trusting the Law-*Giver*.

Now, Jesus is *not* saying that external behavior does not matter. In fact, He is saying that it deeply matters. But He is also saying that for external behavior to have true spiritual currency, it must come from a place of inner renovation that results from "abid[ing] in Me," as Jesus puts it elsewhere. Or as James (2:18) says, "But someone will say, 'You have faith, and I have works.' Show me your faith apart from works, and I by my works will show you faith."

Remember, before these parables, Jesus spends much time making demands and claims on the lives of His followers. In Matthew 5–7, He gives instruction on being righteous in our marriages, sexual desires, speech, responses to enemies, generosity, prayers, fasting, attitudes toward money, judgments, relationships to power, and more. Behavior does matter, according to Jesus.

But for these behaviors to be acceptable to God, they must be the byproduct of God's inner work. Jesus knows that this is the only way for our behavior to be spiritual in any true sense.

Genuine spiritual behavior can only be birthed in and through the Spirit of God. This way is narrow.

Jesus is clear that there are those who would rather trust in their own ability or strength. Most choose that path, which is why it is broad. Worst of all, there will be some who believe they have gone through the narrow gate but find out too late that they were mistaken.

What if Robert had decided that he didn't need any help? If his younger friend Wesley could do it, why, so could he! Flying a plane couldn't be *that* hard, could it? But if he hadn't been able to figure it out on his own, Robert most certainly wouldn't get the chance for a do-over.

Naturally, this life-or-death element of Jesus's teaching ought to jolt us to investigate our own hearts and lives, asking God, "Which gate have I entered through?"

Genuine spiritual behavior can only be birthed in and through the Spirit of God. This way is narrow.

When I was eleven years old, my family moved from Dallas, Texas, to a small town in Virginia's Shenandoah Valley, where my father would pastor a church. Shortly after our family joined this church, we attended the annual Halloween celebration, or as it was known then, "Hallelujah Night." (Like many other churches at this time, ours baptized an "evil" holiday so that its children could dress up in costumes and eat candy like everyone else.)

Still new to the church, my parents decided to dress up like rednecks—fitting with our Texas roots. Their fake teeth, accents, wardrobe, and word choices were above par for being a disguise. They played the part well. The problem was that they played the part a little *too* well. No one knew who they were—at least not until my parents revealed their true identities.

The truth of the matter is that some people are quite good at disguising their true selves. Following His discussion of gates, Jesus makes this exact point when talking about false prophets. Not surprisingly, He uses two more sets of images: sheep and wolves and trees and fruit. He tells His disciples to beware of false prophets who disguise themselves as sheep yet in actuality are vicious wolves. And the only way to identify them, He says, is by the "fruit" that grows on their "trees"—fruit being the outward manifestation of what is on the inside—their output, as it were.

What if Robert had heard another voice on the radio that fateful day offering different instructions? Perhaps this other voice would have given him easier tasks to follow. "Just switch over to autopilot, Robert. The plane can land itself. You can sit back and relax." That would have been tempting, I'm sure. But the results of that false teaching would have been disastrous.

Throughout the Old and New Testaments, we find warnings of false teachers and prophets. Typically, we assume that these false teachers and prophets are easy to identify. But this is not what Jesus says. False teachers, He explains, will often be those who appear righteous but are not. Just because someone prophesies, works miracles, or even casts out evil spirits in His name does not mean they are counted among the good trees.

In fact, any prophet, apostle, preacher, or healing minister who hopes to appear as righteous and innocent as a sheep, yet viciously manipulates hearts, wallets, or emotions for their own sake, are *wolves*. It doesn't matter what their miracle working, healing ministry, or charismatic preaching may look like. As Jesus said, their fruit will reveal if they really "know" Him.

My two oldest kids are at ages at which they love playing games in the pool. On a recent vacation, I spent a lot of time playing with them in the pool at our hotel. Their favorite game was one in which I was a shark that would attack their "boats" (pool floats). Another favorite is the classic Marco Polo, which we also played. And I believe our experience with this call-and-response game illustrates how we are to follow Jesus's instructions.

As followers of Jesus, we are commissioned to live a call-and-response life. When He calls, we must answer. To put it another way, we must hear *and* obey Him. This is what enables us to produce good, lasting fruit. According to Jesus, whether fruit is good or not is measured solely by whether the "producer" hears and obeys His call.

Jesus reinforces this point about fruit by also talking about *foundations* (vv. 24–27).

> Everyone, then, who hears these words of mine and acts on them will be like a wise man who built his house on rock. The rain fell, the floods came, and the winds blew and beat on that house, but it did not fall because it had been founded on rock. And everyone who hears these words of mine and does not act on them will be like a foolish man who built his house on sand. The rain fell, and the floods came, and the winds blew and beat against that house, and it fell—and great was its fall!

Jesus, like the experienced pilot, essentially says, "My teaching is solid and stable. It is trustworthy. It will stand the test of time. Those who ignore it and seek to establish their life on anything else will see their life ultimately swept away." The warnings issued by Jesus are of critical importance and demand our attention. Given that the consequences are a matter of life and death, these commands are not merely for contemplation but for urgent action!

Again, like the broad and narrow gates, the discussions centered around fruit and foundations ought to move us to ask ourselves some difficult questions: *Am I living a life that produces good fruit? Am I obeying Jesus's commands? Or am I simply hearing them without acting on them? What about the foundation of my life? Am I in danger of building my life on the sand of this world, which will eventually leave me homeless? Or have I rooted my inner joys and concerns in the unshakable kingdom of God?*

Even if we do enter the right gate, produce the right fruit, and build upon the right foundation, we may still experience some rough patches. Jesus makes it pretty clear that the path ahead might be difficult. He doesn't sugarcoat it. We might, like Robert, encounter uncertainty and even a rough landing here and there.

But in spite of the struggle, we can rest and trust because we are not on that journey alone. We are following the One who opened the gate and paved the path. And He enables us to begin building our lives on solid ground. Though tough at times, it is in the end the safest route to travel because we follow Him who not only knows the way but who is indeed *the* Way.

Ultimately, we know that many of the listeners in Jesus's day made their choice to enter the wide gate—to go the easy way. They listened to the false prophets. They ignored the voice of the true Prophet, Jesus. They chose to build their lives on sand rather than the Rock. They heard Jesus's words, but they did not respond.

According to Jesus, if they had loved Him, they would have obeyed Him. As Dallas Willard once put it, "For almost two millennia we have heard him. . . . But we have chosen to not do what He said."

This world is on its merry way to a disastrous crash landing. You can choose to go down with it, or you can listen to Jesus and do what He says. Which do you choose?

Though tough at times, it is in the end the safest route to travel because we follow Him who not only knows the way but who is indeed *the* Way.

For Reflection or Discussion

1. Jesus speaks of narrow and wide gates. Reflect on your daily choices and their alignment with either the path to life or the path to destruction. Can you identify any recent times when you consciously chose the narrow gate because of your faith?

2. How does Jesus's teaching on righteousness that goes beyond that of the Pharisees' challenge your understanding of what it means to live a righteous life? Are you outwardly conforming in any ways without the inward transformation of true righteousness?

3. Jesus emphasizes that our actions must stem from a place of inner renovation. How does this perspective shift the way you approach spiritual disciplines and behaviors? Do you feel called to make any changes in your heart to align your external behavior with internal transformation?

4. Jesus warned of false prophets who appear as sheep but are actually wolves. Reflect on your ability to discern truth from

deception in teachings, messages, and other influences in your life. How can you strengthen your discernment to recognize and resist counterfeit guidance?

5. Jesus concludes with the parable of building one's house on the rock rather than on the sand. In practical terms, what does building your life on the rock of Jesus's teachings look like for you today? What shaky areas of your life need to be stabilized?

Standing and Falling

THE STORIES THAT MAKE US

Standing and Falling

The Parable of the Wheat and the Weeds

Matthew 13:24–30

He put before them another parable: "The kingdom of heaven may be compared to someone who sowed good seed in his field; but while everybody was asleep, an enemy came and sowed weeds among the wheat, and then went away. So when the plants came up and bore grain, then the weeds appeared as well. And the slaves of the householder came and said to him, 'Master, did you not sow good seed in your field? Where, then, did these weeds come from?' He answered, 'An enemy has done this.' The slaves said to him, 'Then do you want us to go and gather them?' But he replied, 'No; for in gathering the weeds you would uproot the wheat along with them. Let both of them grow together until the harvest; and at harvest time I will tell the reapers, Collect the weeds first and bind them in bundles to be burned, but gather the wheat into my barn.' "

THE STORIES THAT MAKE US

2

GROWING TOGETHER

In a TED Talk on storytelling, American film director, screenwriter, producer, and voice actor at Pixar, Andrew Stanton, says this:

> Storytelling always leads to a singular goal, and ideally confirming some truth that deepens our understandings of who we are as human beings. We all love stories. We're born for them. Stories affirm who we are. We all want affirmations that our lives have meaning. And nothing gives a greater affirmation than when we connect through stories. It can cross the barriers of time, past, present, and future, and allow us to experience the similarities between ourselves and through others, real and imagined.

Stanton *knows* story. He has worked on such influential films that have captured people's imaginations as *A Bug's Life*, *Toy Story*, *Finding Nemo*, and many others. Toward the end of his talk, he lets us in on his secret for telling a successful story, which is to "use what you know [and] draw from it."

Jesus knew this secret too.

One example of rich storytelling is that of the rabbinic parable from Jewish culture. Jesus—and other Hebrew rabbis of old—crafted simple stories that drove home messages about "God and God's relationship to every human being," as Brad H. Young describes in his book about parables. Often, the truth embedded within the parable may be difficult to discern. But that is intentional; Jesus's parables are meant to be chewed on.

While straightforward, cut-and-dried teachings may be easier to process, truth embedded within a story can be even more profound and potent when sought out and discovered. For example, the Pixar movie *Inside Out* delves into the complex world of emotions within a young girl named Riley. Through the personification of core emotions—Joy, Sadness, Anger, Fear, and Disgust—the movie explores the importance of acknowledging and expressing one's feelings.

Like Jesus's parabolic teachings, *Inside Out* uses a relatable story to convey deep truths about human nature and emotional health. Its viewers are encouraged to reflect on their own emotional experiences and the importance of empathy and understanding. Like the parables, *Inside Out* invites its audience to dig deeper, beyond the surface-level enjoyment of the film, to uncover the insightful messages about life and human nature set within its narrative.

Jesus was the master of this same kind of multilayered, thought-provoking storytelling. We know from the Gospels that Jesus liked sharing radical truths through story. In fact, Young also points out that "one-third of the recorded sayings of Jesus in [Matthew, Mark, and Luke] are in parables"!

One of Jesus's stories, commonly known as the Parable of the Wheat and the Weeds, contains a deeper meaning that must be unwrapped and interpreted.

As Andrew Stanton said, one of the best tactics when telling a story is to use what you know. And in this parable, Jesus uses what He and His listeners knew well: agriculture. Even if his listeners were not all farmers, they would have understood what it took to produce food—some seed, some soil, some sun, and some rain. Agriculture had all the makings of a fertile metaphor for Jesus when He taught about the kingdom of God.

In the Parable of the Wheat and the Weeds in Matthew 13:24–30, Jesus tells about a farmer who plants wheat in his field. But that night, as he and his workers sleep, his enemy comes and plants weeds among the wheat and then slips away undetected. When the crop begins to grow, the weeds also grow. And so, when the farmer's workers notice the weeds, they report the finding to the farmer.

The farmer wisely discerns that his enemy planted the weeds. However, rather than asking his workers to pull up the weeds, the farmer tells them to let the weeds and the wheat grow together until the time of the harvest.

Those hearing this story firsthand would have understood that farmers and landowners depend on the quality of their crops. Certainly, an enemy sowing weeds into their fields would have ruined a business. But what the hearers might not have recognized at first is how Jesus's story relates to the kingdom of God. Fortunately for His disciples—and for us—Jesus later explains the parable when He is alone with them. And we, like a good farmer, must dig a little deeper to uncover its hidden essence.

In verse 36, the conversation turns from public to private. Jesus goes from telling a story to the crowds that followed Him to divulging the meaning behind the story to His closest friends.

Not too long ago, my wife, Anna, and I caught up with some old friends over dinner. This couple was telling us how they'd had to learn to navigate their differing temperaments and personalities during their early years of marriage.

The wife told us that in those newlywed days, her husband would disagree with her in front of their parents and other family members. She, who is much more private, would then give him "the look." (If any of you reading this are husbands, I'm sure you've gotten "the look" before.)

Well, after our friend had received "the look" several times, it began to sink in that he needed to practice more discretion during their disagreements. He eventually discovered that what was best for their relationship was to work out their problems in private. See, she preferred to hash out their arguments when the two of them were alone, not in front of others.

But a lot of this issue derived from their different upbringings. In his family, it was common and even natural to have out marital disputes around other people. However, in her family, such quarrels were private. But what they learned together is that no matter their upbringing, some things are best discussed in private rather than in public.

In this passage of scripture, we see just that: Jesus moves from a public to a private setting to share more intimate details about His stories with those He is closest to. Jesus leaves the crowds and retreats into a house, where he instructs the disciples privately in response to their request for an explanation of the parable. He tells them that He had been speaking metaphorically, and He interprets the metaphors in verses 37–39, calling Himself the Son of Man:

The one who sows the good seed is the Son of Man; the field is the world, and the good seed are the children of the kingdom; the weeds are the children of the evil one, and the enemy who sowed them is the devil; the harvest is the end of the age, and the reapers are angels.

By listening to Jesus, we find out *who* and *what* He is talking about.

In the history of Israel prior to Jesus's birth, the Jewish people had been exiled from their land and scattered throughout the Mediterranean world. In this way, God's people, the Jews, are the wheat—the good seed—who were planted by God in the field, which is the world. The wheat is scattered throughout the field, which is the exiled Jews dispersed throughout the world.

Yet the enemy, the devil, has also planted weeds among the wheat in the field. And even Jesus encountered these weeds! These were the ones who opposed Jesus and His ministry. Therefore, the wheat, as a result of the weeds, grow weary and discouraged.

We can certainly relate to that today, which again shows the brilliance of Jesus's storytelling, according to Andrew Stanton's formula. We see the weeds wreaking havoc in the field. We see the harm being done to the wheat. God's people long for the harvest, and they have been waiting now for thousands of years.

Without question, this metaphor would have connected with Jesus's disciples. Jesus was with them in His human form, and they were awaiting Him to be made king and to set things right. And just like us, they yearned for the day that Jesus would deal with the weeds and collect the wheat to Himself.

At one point in the Gospels, two of Jesus's disciples, James and John, ask Jesus to do them a favor in the future and allow them to sit next to Him when He is on His throne—one on His right and one on His left. They were ready to see the wheat exalted and the weeds burned up! For too long, it had looked like the Lord was sitting by, allowing the weeds to infect the field and smother the wheat instead of plucking them out.

Surely, these faithful Jews had sung the lament of David in Psalm 13:1–2:

> How long, O Lord? Will you forget me forever?
>   How long will you hide your face from me?
> How long must I bear pain in my soul,
>   and have sorrow in my heart all day long?
> How long shall my enemy be exalted over me?

For too long, it looked like the Lord had been hanging back while the weeds grew and prospered. It looked like the weeds would eventually choke out the wheat and take over. Years and years had dragged on; promises had been made. But there seemed to be no action, no word, no rescue. Only deafening silence and the sprouting of more and more weeds.

This is where, like in the movie *Inside Out*, we can relate this message to our personal lives. Have you experienced seasons of silence before? I don't know about you, but this sounds like situations I have walked through and likely, at some point, will walk through again. We all at one time or another will want to cry out, "God, why are You allowing this? When will You do something?"

Have you been there before? Maybe you are even in this place today. If so, allow Jesus's message to take root in your soul.

He says to His disciples—to us—"Don't grow weary. The harvest is coming. Don't give up. Don't allow frustration, pain, or disillusionment to move you away from trust; allow it to thrust you *into* trust. Because the harvest is coming, and the wheat and the weeds will be sorted."

See the promise in the parable in the day it was spoken: Though the enemy and the weeds he has planted are having their heyday now, Jesus has come to cast them out. Through His life, coming death, and coming resurrection, Jesus is defeating the devil and his weeds. The harvest has broken into time through Jesus. The time has come. And yet. . . .

Although Christ has come and judgment is nearing, the harvest has also come and is not yet fully here.

> Although Christ has come and judgment is nearing, the harvest has also come and is not yet fully here.

I remember when Anna and I bought our first house. It was thrilling to be a homeowner at last. About a month before our first child, Adelaide, was born, we signed the papers, put a down payment on the house, and moved in. The down payment, of course, was only a part of the full price paid at the time of purchase. Although we said it was "our house," it was also in a sense the *bank's* house. The down payment and our monthly mortgage payments would help us move toward a future in which the house was totally and completely ours. And yet, it wasn't fully in our grasp.

In a similar way, Jesus bought His people a promise. This promise—of the judgment of the weeds and the glorification of the wheat—has been bought by Jesus's death and resurrection. And so it is assured! We *own* this promise because God has gifted it to us. He has given us His Spirit with the down payment of God's promise.

But Jesus's coming again is what will bring the balance so that we can finally see all the rewards of owning this promise. It is a promise that is coming for those who, like paying that mortgage month after month, patiently trust in God through the thick and thin.

We *own* this promise because God has gifted it to us. He has given us His Spirit with the down payment of God's promise.

After Jesus's ascension into heaven, the Apostle Peter writes this to a community of believers who are being persecuted for their faith (2 Peter 3:8–9):

> But do not ignore this one fact, beloved, that with the Lord one day is like a thousand years, and a thousand years are like one day. The Lord is not slow about his promise, as some think of slowness, but is patient with you, not wanting any to perish, but all to come to repentance.

For those who represent the wheat in this parable, the time between the promise and the fulfillment of that promise can feel like forever. The wait can be painful. But this is why we call following Jesus a life of faith. Our faith is in Jesus, who is trustworthy and who always makes good on His promises, even when it seems He is being slow.

Though we may want to, we must remember that we cannot prematurely separate the wheat and the weeds. It is not yet time. The "sorting out" cannot take place too early because the Lord is giving the weeds time to repent. Furthermore—and this point is crucial—it is not our field to harvest. The harvest belongs to God.

So what does this mean for you and me? Today, we must trust that God is the one who is best able to judge between the weeds and the wheat and will do so at the best time—the time of the harvest. No matter how often we like to trick ourselves into thinking we are in charge and in complete control of our lives, this parable reminds us that God is the Farmer. It is His field and His harvest. He alone will do the judging and the sorting out.

But we like to climb onto the judge's bench, don't we? When we find ourselves in these places where things need sorting out and we want to do the sorting ourselves, we must repent of that urge. We must move away from *controlling* and toward patiently *trusting* in God and His perfect timing.

As Peter says, God is not slow. Like a good farmer, He is patient. And God's patience is rooted in His desire for more weeds to be remade into wheat. He is patient because of His infinite love for all of us. He wants *none* to perish.

Incredibly, this isn't just for the weeds' sake but also for the wheat's sake.

How is God's patience good for the faithful as well? If we look closely at this parable and what it means in our lives, we will see that "belief and unbelief—like the wheat and the weeds in the parable—are mixed together in each one of us," as author José A. Pagola says.

Though we may be essentially wheat, we still have weeds in us that God wants to pull up. He wants to make us more and more into His image (2 Corinthians 3:18).

I don't know about you, but for me, it is a lot easier to see the weeds in other people's lives than it is my own! But this is why Jesus says this in Matthew 7:1–5:

> Do not judge, so that you may not be judged. For with the judgment you make you will be judged, and the measure

you give will be the measure you get. Why do you see the speck in your neighbor's eye, but do not notice the log in your own eye? Or how can you say to your neighbor, "Let me take the speck out of your eye," while the log is in your own eye? You hypocrite, first take the log out of your own eye, and then you will see clearly to take the speck out of your neighbor's eye.

We need to ask ourselves, *Am I putting myself in the judgment seat?* It is a constant temptation of the faithful—to judge the unfaithful. It is so easy to become proud and even secretly scorn others in our own hearts. But the Apostle Paul warns us that this is poison for our souls (Romans 2:1–5, 16):

> Therefore you have no excuse, whoever you are, when you judge others; for in passing judgment on another you condemn yourself, because you, the judge, are doing the very same things. You say, "We know that God's judgment on those who do such things is in accordance with truth." Do you imagine, whoever you are, that when you judge those who do such things and yet do them yourself, you will escape the judgment of God? Or do you despise the riches of his kindness and forbearance and patience? Do you not realize that God's kindness is meant to lead you to repentance? But by your hard and impenitent heart you are storing up wrath for yourself on the day of wrath, when God's righteous judgment will be revealed . . . on the day when, according to my gospel, God, through Jesus Christ, will judge the secret thoughts of all.

The reason that we are told not to judge is because we all *already* have a Judge. When we judge, we put ourselves in a position that only God can fill. The reason that we can rest when we are wronged is because we know that one day these wrongs will be made right by the perfect Judge.

Now, as an aside, there is a difference between judging *someone* and judging between what is right and what is wrong. We can discern whether an action is right or wrong without moving into the self-righteous and precarious judgment of a person. But it is a fine line, and I think more often than not, we can so easily cross the line into the judgment of others without even realizing it because we are so accustomed to doing so.

But the point Paul is making is that even the faithful deal with unfaithfulness. So instead of judging the world, we should instead examine the fields of our own lives and pray for our hearts to be transformed into God's heart for the lost weeds.

I believe this parable also teaches us the importance of faith. When people say, "Just have faith," it can sound like faith is simply sticking your head in the sand—forgetting there is a problem or ignoring a true reality that we are grappling with.

But that is not the kind of faith that Jesus talks about. Biblically, faith is patient trust in God. True, God does not weed out the field as quickly as we wish or think He should! But the kingdom of God is unhurried, on pace, and in comparison to our timelines, *slow*.

We too often think like Abraham and Sarah in the book of Genesis. God promised Abraham that Sarah would give birth to their son, Isaac. But instead of believing God and waiting for the promise to come about, Abraham conceived Ishmael with Sarah's slave, Hagar.

This is an apt picture of our impatient human nature. We have the word that God will bring about a promise, but when it takes longer than we think it should, we look for quick fixes. We take control. And in doing so, like Abraham, we create problematic situations with Hagars and Ishmaels (Genesis 16:1–4). Before we know it, we have short-circuited our own lives in the process.

Instead of rushing to do the Farmer's job for Him—pulling the weeds or reaping the harvest or plowing up the whole field—we must, like a wise farmer, embrace patient trust. That doesn't mean we just wait patiently for God to *do* something; we patiently *trust*, which means we trust God's word to us more than we trust our sense of what seems to be going on.

Let's face it: Sometimes it looks like the harvest will never come. Sometimes it looks like the Farmer has abandoned His field and is letting the weeds take over. We are quick to look around us and assume that God is gone or given up.

But through the eyes of true faith, through the eyes of patient trust, through eyes that trust in the God of resurrection and redemption—He has not abandoned us or His field. God is on the move. And He always makes good on His promises.

For Reflection or Discussion

1. How are you like the wheat, showing growth and positive contributions to the kingdom of God? Conversely, what "weeds" have cropped up in your life that may need addressing or removing to foster better growth?

2. Where in your life do you need to trust more in God's timing and less in your own desire for immediate resolution or justice?

3. Considering a situation in which you are currently waiting, how might cultivating patience and trust in God's timing change your approach and attitude during this period?

4. Regarding both wheat and weeds growing together until the harvest, how do you view the role of suffering or challenges in your life? Do you see them as opportunities for growth and deepening your faith?

5. How does the parable challenge your tendency to judge others? In what ways can you be more gracious and patient, recognizing that transformation is a process and that, like the wheat and the weeds, it is not your place to separate or judge?

THE STORIES THAT MAKE US

Growing Together

The Parable of the Unmerciful Servant

Matthew 18:21–35

Then Peter came and said to him, "Lord, if another member of the church sins against me, how often should I forgive? As many as seven times?" Jesus said to him, "Not seven times, but, I tell you, seventy-seven times.

"For this reason the kingdom of heaven may be compared to a king who wished to settle accounts with his slaves. When he began the reckoning, one who owed him ten thousand talents was brought to him; and, as he could not pay, his lord ordered him to be sold, together with his wife and children and all his possessions, and payment to be made. So the slave fell on his knees before him, saying, 'Have patience with me, and I will pay you everything.' And out of pity for him, the lord of that slave released him and forgave him the debt. But that same slave, as he went out, came upon one of his fellow slaves who owed him a hundred denarii; and seizing him by the throat, he said, 'Pay what you owe.' Then his fellow slave fell down and pleaded with him, 'Have patience with me, and I will pay you.' But he refused; then he went and threw him into prison until he would pay the debt. When his fellow slaves saw what had happened, they were greatly distressed, and they went and reported to their lord all that had taken place. Then his lord summoned him and said to him, 'You wicked slave! I forgave you all that debt because you pleaded with me. Should you not have had mercy on your fellow slave, as I had mercy on you?' And in anger his lord handed him over to be tortured until he would pay his entire debt. So my heavenly Father will also do to every one of you if you do not forgive your brother or sister from your heart."

THE STORIES THAT MAKE US

3

FORGIVEN BUT UNFORGIVING

We've all heard the old saying "Do as I say, not as I do." When someone utters these words, they mean to say, "Follow my instructions, *not* my example." It implies that the one using the maxim makes mistakes, and so one should take their advice rather than emulate their actions.

As a parent, I have had too many unfortunate opportunities to use this saying. I remember when my oldest daughter, Adelaide, got angry and called her little sister, Audrey, a "fool." This was uncharacteristic of Adelaide. I corrected her, telling her that it was not appropriate to call her sister a fool.

"Name-calling accomplishes nothing," I said. Then I asked her where she had even heard the word *fool*.

She didn't hesitate. "Daddy, I heard you call Lola a fool when you got mad at her."

Whoops. Lola is our sweet, lovable, yet stubborn beagle.

So in that teachable (for both of us) moment, I simply said, "Adelaide, do as I say, not as I do—"

No, I'm kidding. Actually, I told her that I had been wrong to call Lola a fool and I was sorry for setting a bad example.

The problem with this maxim—"do as I say, not as I do"—is that it makes its user a total hypocrite. And it's even more problematic for Christians, who are supposed to be a people whose actions match our instructions. In 1 Corinthians 11:1, Paul boldly tells the church of Corinth, "Be imitators of me, as I am of Christ." Or in other words, "Follow my example, as I follow the example of Christ" (NIV).

As we follow Jesus, we invoke others to follow us. In our secular culture, a Christian's personal life might be the only witness for Christ some people ever see—the only Bible those watching ever read. And so we must ask ourselves: *Are we living in such a way that we could say, as Paul says, "Follow my example, as I follow the example of Christ"?*

I want to ask this question in a specific way that might sting: Are we following the example of Christ in how we forgive others?

To quote Hamlet, "Ay, there's the rub."

Jesus tells a story (a parable) to His disciples after Peter asks this question in Matthew 18:21: "Lord, if another member of the church sins against me, how often should I forgive? As many as seven times?"

We'll get to the parable in a moment. But first, Jesus replies to Peter, "You fool—"

Nope, just kidding again. Thankfully, Jesus is much more patient with Peter (and us) than I am with my dog Lola! Instead, He replies, "Not seven times, but, I tell you, seventy-seven times."

We can catch the basic point here without much effort: Jesus wants us to forgive much more than Peter wants to. But to get to the real essence of what Jesus is saying, we need to look at the numbers *seven* and *seventy-seven*.

In scripture, numbers are often important, and these numbers so being point to a deeper meaning—one beyond quantity. Interestingly, seven is a number that carries deep significance in scripture. In fact, according to the *Dictionary of Biblical Imagery*, "of the numbers that carry symbolic meaning . . . seven is the most important. It is used to signify *completeness*."

Without going into too much detail, here is a brief sketch of how the number seven is used in the New Testament to indicate completeness:

- There are seven "signs" of Jesus in the book of John.
- There are seven parables in Matthew 13.
- There are seven churches in Revelation 2–4.
- There are seven characteristics of wisdom in James 3:17.

And let's not forget, this pattern begins in the Genesis creation account in which there are six days of work and a seventh day that is saved for Sabbath rest.

And so, here in Matthew 18, Peter borrows from this tradition when he asks his question. He thinks, "Surely, seven is the 'complete' or 'perfect' answer for forgiveness!" Jesus, as He often does, surprises Peter.

He surprises *us* too. Forgiving someone seven times sounds incredibly generous to me. If someone were to wrong me seven times in a short amount of time, I would probably think it best to avoid that person!

But Jesus replies to Peter in an unexpected way: He tells His followers, then and now, to forgive *seventy-seven* times. If seven represents completeness, or fullness, seventy-seven represents *immeasurable* completeness. Or put another way, Jesus is saying, "Your forgiveness should be unlimited."

But this isn't where Jesus's creativity ends. If we are familiar with the whole of scripture, including the Old Testament, we can hear echoes in Jesus's answer of the story of Lamech in Genesis 4.

Lamech was a descendant of Cain. And if you know the story of Cain and Abel, the first siblings, you know that Cain killed his brother Abel. Abel had done him no wrong, but out of pure jealousy, Cain killed his brother. As a result of his sin, God banished Cain from his land. And so Cain left and established a city "founded on the blood of an innocent brother," says Leithart.

Lamech, coming from Cain's family line years later, tells his wives this in Genesis 4:23–24:

> Adah and Zillah, hear my voice;
> you wives of Lamech, listen to what I say:
> I have killed a man for wounding me,
> a young man for striking me.
> If Cain is avenged sevenfold,
> truly Lamech seventy-sevenfold.

Lamech, having murdered a young man, follows in the footsteps of his ancestor Cain. And he uses the numbers seven and seventy-seven in the context of *vengeance*. But then Jesus, when answering Peter's question, uses these same numbers in the context of *forgiveness*. And we can be sure that Jesus, who was indeed familiar with the books of Moses, not to mention the history of the world, is purposefully referencing this event in Genesis.

Lamech uses these numbers to describe his city, which is marked by unlimited vengeance. But Jesus uses these same numbers to cast the vision of another city, or kingdom, marked by unlimited forgiveness. Though our own cities may be characterized by vengeance, Jesus's heavenly city—what He calls the "kingdom of God"—is characterized by forgiveness. In Jesus's kingdom, wrongs are made right, unfairness is evened out, debts are canceled, and obligations are released.

This is to say that Jesus's kingdom is quite different from the kinds of places we are used to living in. In a world of Lamechs, we are charged to become Peters.

Jesus commissions us to be the kind of people whose first thought is not "How can I get even?" but rather "How can I forgive in love?" But as we know from experience, this is not in any way easy. Thankfully, Jesus provides us His example to follow, and His parable shows us how.

In the story Jesus tells after shocking Peter with His answer, we find a servant who owes the king a tremendous sum of money. This would be considered millions of dollars today, and the servant cannot repay it. When he begs the king to be patient with him, the king mercifully forgives his debt.

Jesus says that immediately after the servant is forgiven, he encounters a fellow servant who owes him a few thousand dollars. Compared to the debt the first servant was just forgiven, this amount is measly and fully repayable. But when the debtor makes the very same plea the forgiven servant had made to the king, his reaction is not one of forgiveness but of retribution. He has the unfortunate fellow servant tortured and imprisoned. This forgiven servant is not only cruel but also a complete hypocrite.

As Anna Case-Winters says, "This servant with the astronomical, unrepayable debt receives astonishingly gracious forgiveness from the debt from a King. Yet, when the tables are turned, and the servant has a chance to be gracious, he seems to know nothing of grace."

THE STORIES THAT MAKE US

Nothing strikes fear in the heart of a person quite like the sound of a siren and the sight of flashing lights in the rearview mirror. Being pulled over by a cop is no fun—unless, perhaps, you find yourself in a scenario straight out of *Super Troopers* or *Police Academy*. But outside of those absurd, comedic situations, it's no fun, right?

Once, a police officer pulled a driver over and asked for his license and registration. The driver asked, "What's wrong, officer? I didn't go through any red lights, and I certainly wasn't speeding."

"No, you weren't," said the officer. "*But* I saw you waving your fist as you swerved around the lady driving in the left lane, and I further observed your flushed and angry face as you shouted at the driver of the Hummer that cut you off, and how you pounded your steering wheel when the traffic came to a stop near the bridge."

"I don't understand," the driver said. "Is that a crime?"

"No, but when I saw the 'Jesus loves you and so do I' bumper sticker on the car, I figured this car had to be stolen."

Cheesy? Perhaps. But the simple truth is that all humans—including Christians—can slip into the easy trap of hypocrisy. Again, we are more used to embodying the "do I as I say, not as I do" mantra. By presenting the hypocrisy of the forgiven servant who acted unforgiving, Jesus exposes our hypocrisy when it comes to forgiving others in our own lives.

True, Jesus's calling out of our hypocrisy isn't overly sweet or grandfatherly. He comes with a stern rebuke and warning that might be a bit shocking to us:

> Then his lord summoned him and said to him, "You wicked slave! I forgave you all that debt because you pleaded with

me. Should you not have had mercy on your fellow slave, as I had mercy on you?" And in anger his lord handed him over to be tortured until he would pay his entire debt. So my heavenly Father will also do to every one of you if you do not forgive your brother or sister from your heart.

No doubt this passage is chilling, especially the last part. The parable and its moral suggest that God's mercy will turn to wrath if we do not forgive one another.

Jesus isn't messing around here. He essentially says, "Do you want to end up being tortured? Do you want to have to pay every last penny you owe? Then by all means, keep your vengeance. Hold your grudge. Hang on to your petty anger." According to Jesus, unforgiveness is the path to hell.

Now I will admit, as I typed these words in my study, I cringed. I felt convicted. Not only because I realize I still have my own unforgiveness that I need to release to God but also because I was reminded that the sin of unforgiveness goes much deeper than we may think. Unforgiveness is the sin of idolatry, first and foremost. It is the sin of the Garden—Adam and Eve wanting to be like God, the Judge over all.

One theologian, Karl Barth, notes this very fact: that original sin is rooted in our desire to be the judge of our fellow humans:

> All sin has its being and origin in the fact that man wants to be his own judge. And in wanting to be that, and thinking and acting accordingly, he and his whole world is in conflict with God.

Unforgiveness is the sin of idolatry, first and foremost. It is the sin of the Garden.

Let me explain something about forgiveness: It isn't letting people off the hook. It is, however, letting our desire for judgment go and placing it in the Judge's hands. It is taking ourselves off the throne and allowing God to be God. It is our opportunity to stop pretending to be something we are not. Ultimately, as Peter Leithart says, "Forgiveness is a confession that judgment belongs to the Lord."

So often we struggle to let go of unforgiveness and bitterness because we lack an understanding of God as Judge. We sometimes seem to prefer a domesticated or tame God who does not judge. Perhaps this is not because God as Judge is a scary concept but rather because we would prefer to swap roles with God. We would prefer to sit in the judgment seat and let God be the ultimate forgiver.

But no. That's not the way the story goes. We have been told to forgive seventy-seven times and allow God to handle justice as only He can. He is the merciful and just Judge. In fact, it is *only* God who can rightly be both merciful and just in judgment.

We shouldn't fool ourselves. We are incapable of perfect judgment. Instead, we must forgive and allow God to be God.

Jesus, in His wisdom, knows that forgiveness is the path to human flourishing. Miroslav Volf, a Christian theologian at Yale, puts it this way:

> But our actions are irreversible.... And so the urge for vengeance seems irrepressible.... The only way out ... is through *forgiveness*.... A genuinely free act which "does not merely re-act," forgiveness breaks the power of the remembered past ... and so makes the spiral of vengeance grind to a halt.

Forgiveness not only makes us right with God but also with others. In this way, forgiveness fulfills what Jesus told His disciples were the two greatest commandments: love of God and love of others.

> We would prefer to sit in the judgment seat and let God be the ultimate forgiver.

Author Rebecca Pippert had the opportunity to audit some graduate-level courses at Harvard University, one of which was titled "Systems of Counseling." During one class, the professor presented a case study in which therapeutic methods were used to help a man uncover a deep hostility and anger toward his mother. This helped the client understand himself in new ways that then enabled him to begin to move on.

However, Pippert, who was auditing the course, then asked the professor how he would have responded if the man had asked for help to forgive his mother. The professor responded that forgiveness was a concept that assumed moral responsibility and many other things that scientific psychology could not speak to.

"Don't force your values . . . about forgiveness onto the patient," he said.

When some of the students responded with dismay, the professor tried to relieve the tension with some humor. "If you guys are looking for a changed heart, I think you are looking in the wrong department."

This particular exchange stuck with Pippert. Reflecting on that conversation, she makes this important point: "The truth is, we are looking for a changed heart."

Though I believe psychology and psychotherapy can be helpful, they cannot, as Tim Keller says, give us any basis for a deep and powerful message of forgiveness and redemption. The truth is, forgiveness—and a changed heart, for that matter—can only come through the power of the Spirit of Jesus Christ. And the reason we forgive is in response to God's forgiveness of us: "Be kind to one another, tenderhearted, forgiving one another, as God in Christ has forgiven you" (Ephesians 4:32).

Because God has forgiven us, we must forgive others. This isn't a suggestion but a command. God isn't telling us to do as He says not as He does. He has forgiven us an astronomical debt. And we are to do not only as He says but also as He does.

In fact, this parable, along with other sayings of Jesus, suggests that our forgiveness is in some sense dependent upon our forgiveness of others: "Whenever you stand praying, forgive, if you have anything against anyone; so that your Father in heaven may also forgive you your trespasses" (Mark 11:25). Similarly, the writer of 1 John says this to his community: "*If* we confess our sins, he is faithful and just and will forgive us our sins and purify us from all unrighteousness" (1:9, emphasis mine).

These scriptures imply a connection between our own forgiveness and our forgiveness of others. Yet how do we understand this in light of the Apostle Paul's statement about God forgiving us while we were still in sin and did nothing to deserve it? (See Romans 5:8.)

Perhaps it is best to say that like the servant in the parable, we don't deserve God's forgiveness. And we certainly cannot do anything to deserve it. Yet to abide, or remain, in Christ (John 15:4), we must take on Christ's character of forgiveness. We must follow His example. In this way, we are not *earning* anything; we are abiding and reaping the natural consequences of what it means to follow Christ.

Forgiven but Unforgiving

Writer James Bryan Smith says,

> We will forgive when we know, truly know, we have been, and will be, forgiven by a merciful God. We forgive others when we look at Jesus, our master and model, who willingly humbled himself, took the form of a servant, and gave his very life as a demonstration of forgiveness and reconciliation.

Now, forgiveness isn't the same as reconciliation. In abusive situations, it is best to forgive from afar rather than reconcile. "But how do you forgive?" you might ask.

Smith goes on to give what I think is a brilliant picture of what forgiveness entails:

> We do not merely forgive as the Lord forgave us, not merely because the Lord forgave us, we forgive *with the Lord* [my emphasis]. We can only forgive when we know and feel the presence of Jesus standing with us, the One who is the model but also the means of forgiveness.

Jesus is the "*means* of forgiveness." Put another way, Jesus working through us is the only way we truly can forgive, the only way we can, as Volf said, "break the power of the remembered past." Forgiveness is not something we do in our own strength; it is something that happens by the power of God working in and through us.

As Jesus tells us in Matthew 19, some things are impossible for humanity, but *all* things are possible with God.

For Reflection or Discussion

1. Considering the parable of the unforgiving servant, where might there be inconsistencies in your own life between receiving God's forgiveness and extending forgiveness to others?

2. In what situation(s) have you found it difficult to release your desire for judgment and instead place it in God's hands? How can you work toward letting go of this desire?

3. Reflecting on the astronomical debt forgiven by the king in Jesus's parable, how does this image impact your willingness to forgive debts (not just financial) that others may owe you?

4. Forgiveness is often a journey rather than a one-time action. Reflecting on your own journey, what steps do you need to take to move closer to a posture of heart that forgives freely and fully as Jesus teaches?

5. How can embracing forgiveness in cases of betrayal or abuse, in which reconciliation is not viable, serve as an opportunity for God to work transformative healing within all those involved?

Forgiven but Unforgiving

THE STORIES THAT MAKE US

Forgiven but Unforgiving

The Parable of the Wedding Banquet

Matthew 22:1–14

Once more Jesus spoke to them in parables, saying: "The kingdom of heaven may be compared to a king who gave a wedding banquet for his son. He sent his slaves to call those who had been invited to the wedding banquet, but they would not come. Again he sent other slaves, saying, 'Tell those who have been invited: Look, I have prepared my dinner, my oxen and my fat calves have been slaughtered, and everything is ready; come to the wedding banquet.' But they made light of it and went away, one to his farm, another to his business, while the rest seized his slaves, mistreated them, and killed them. The king was enraged. He sent his troops, destroyed those murderers, and burned their city. Then he said to his slaves, 'The wedding is ready, but those invited were not worthy. Go therefore into the main streets, and invite everyone you find to the wedding banquet.' Those slaves went out into the streets and gathered all whom they found, both good and bad; so the wedding hall was filled with guests.

"But when the king came in to see the guests, he noticed a man there who was not wearing a wedding robe, and he said to him, 'Friend, how did you get in here without a wedding robe?' And he was speechless. Then the king said to the attendants, 'Bind him hand and foot, and throw him into the outer darkness, where there will be weeping and gnashing of teeth.' For many are called, but few are chosen."

THE STORIES THAT MAKE US

4

WEDDING CLOTHES

Following the 2001 animated comedy *Shrek*, its 2004 sequel continues the story of an ogre from a swamp who marries a princess. In *Shrek 2*, the princess Fiona takes her new husband, Shrek, to the kingdom of Far Far Away to meet her royal parents.

The king and queen of Far Far Away receive a shock when they discover that their new son-in-law is a big, green ogre and because of a magic spell, Fiona now looks just like him.

The awkward family sits down to a royal meal at which personalities and prejudices begin to clash. Although it begins politely enough, the king mutters a few thinly veiled insults at his daughter's new husband. As tensions build, the king and Shrek glare at one another from opposite ends of a long, ornate table.

"So I suppose any grandchildren I could expect from you would be. . ." the king begins.

"Ogres, yes," Shrek answers through clenched teeth.

Attempting to keep the peace, the queen assures, "Not that there's anything wrong with that. Right, Harold?"

"No," the king says sarcastically. "That is assuming you don't eat your own young!"

As classical music plays blithely in the background, any illusion of family togetherness is buried under a bombardment of harsh words and grimaces. The anger spreads from husband to wife, as Fiona screams at Shrek and the queen snaps at the king.

Suddenly, the battle breaks out in earnest—the food on the table becoming weapons—completely ruining the feast. The crackers are crushed, the lobster is cracked, Shrek shreds the chicken, the king fillets the fish, and a roasted pig sails high into the air.

Defeated, the queen whimpers, "It's so nice to have the family together for dinner."

Although fictitious and exaggerated, this scene provides an all-too-relatable experience for many of us. Who hasn't sat through an awkward meal before? Who hasn't attended a gathering that didn't include, if not a food fight and outright shouting, at least a bit of tension?

Yet despite these unwelcome incidents, we know that eating with others in most cases can be a healthy and joyous experience. Author Miriam Weinstein, in her book *The Surprising Power of Family Meals*, says, "Sitting down to a meal together . . . encloses us and strengthens the bonds that connect us with other members of our self-defined clan, shutting out the rest of the world."

While shared meals often provide positive experiences and good memories, they may sometimes be difficult, like Shrek and Fiona's confrontation with the king and queen.

Take Jesus's story in Matthew 22; in it, we read about a meal—a wedding feast—with great opposition surrounding it.

Spoiler alert: This wedding is full of turmoil! Sure, every wedding has its share of drama, but this one truly exceeds all expectations. We have wedding guests who murder the people who invited them, a city destroyed because the guests refuse the wedding invitation, and a man who is thrown into "outer darkness" for committing a fashion faux pas. This makes the dinner scene from *Shrek 2* look like a nursery school squabble.

What are we to make of such a story? In seeking to discern the meaning and significance of Jesus's parable, we first need to understand the framework that Jesus is speaking within.

The Parable of the Wedding Banquet is situated within a series of three parables. Jesus tells these three tales following an encounter with religious leaders who are questioning his authority (Matthew 21:23–27). This is important to remember as we explore the story.

Here's a synopsis:

A king prepares a great wedding feast for his son and sends his servants out to notify the guests that the banquet is ready. But the guests who had been invited ignore the invitation. Others seize the messengers and murder them.

The Pharisees, who were the religious leaders of the time, hearing this parable probably recognized that they represent the wedding guests in this story—the invitees who made light of the invitation and even mistreated and killed the messengers sent to invite them.

In other words, the guests invited to the wedding feast are the religious leaders who have ignored Jesus and killed the prophets who tried to tell them who Jesus really is. We can be certain that the Pharisees did not appreciate this parallel!

But the invited guests rejecting the invitation and killing the messengers isn't where the story ends. When the king hears the news, he becomes so furious that he sends out an army to destroy the invitees and burn their city.

Then in verse 8, the story begins to shift. The king tells his servants: "The wedding is ready, but those invited were not worthy. Go therefore into the main streets, and invite everyone you find to the wedding banquet" (vv. 8–9).

So the king's servants bring in everyone they can find to the banquet, and as a result, the hall is filled. Now, what is the parallel here?

The servants being sent out to gather all the people for the feast is representative of Jesus's ministry. Like a princess bringing an ogre husband home to the royal palace, Jesus is bringing so-called "unworthy" people into the king's hall so that they may eat the royal food of the kingdom. Those once deemed unfit and unwelcome are now brought in. This is what Jesus is all about. He came to bring people from the street corners into the kingdom of God.

But then Jesus's story turns yet again in what seems to be an odd direction. The king comes in to meet the guests and notices a man who isn't wearing the proper wedding clothes. And so the king orders his aides to bind the man's hands and feet and throw him into "outer darkness, where there will be weeping and gnashing of teeth."

Here we have a man who has been officially invited to the wedding feast by the king, and he shows up—unlike the first round of guests—only to be kicked out later. In fact, he is bound, hands and feet, and tossed into utter darkness because of his unsuitable wardrobe. What are we to make of that?

More than twelve years ago, Anna and I were married on a hot summer day. Before the reception, we posed outside for a great many photographs, and the wedding party was thoroughly heated by the end of it, including me.

Given the ceremony that had preceded and all of the greeting and dancing that followed at our reception, I was quite ready to be out of my suit by the time the reception began to wind down.

Anna and I had planned to leave the reception a little early. It was my understanding that we would greet all our guests, eat a meal, dance a few numbers, and then slip out. Our guests could keep dancing and eating and having a good time, while we would leave for our honeymoon.

Let's just say that I totally misunderstood the plan.

What happened was this: I said my goodbyes at the reception and, thinking we were going to slip away unseen, changed into something comfortable—basketball shorts and a T-shirt. I was hot and ready to be rid of my suit and, again, thought we were leaving the wedding guests to enjoy the rest of the party.

But then I realized that Anna was still in her wedding dress and I was walking into a formal bride and groom sendoff . . . in basketball shorts and a white undershirt.

People were cheering, blowing bubbles, throwing confetti . . . and *laughing* at me.

There I was, in flip-flops, shorts, and an undershirt, escorting my glamorous bride in her wedding dress. All this is to say that I know firsthand what it means to come to a wedding dressed inappropriately.

In Jesus's story, we find this poor chap in the same situation. He is underdressed for the formal feast, and in this case, his improper wardrobe is a serious offense. It is not as though he is dressed inappropriately because he is too poor or lacks the means to obtain the proper wedding attire.

To get at what is going on here, we have to look at the symbolic meaning of clothing throughout scripture. Clothing symbolizes many things in the New Testament. Consider how Paul addresses the church in Rome (Romans 13:12–14, emphasis mine):

> The night is far gone, the day is near. Let us then lay aside the works of darkness and *put on* [some translations say, "clothe ourselves with"] the armor of light; let us live honorably as in the day, not in reveling and drunkenness, not in debauchery and licentiousness, not in quarreling and jealousy. Instead, *put on* [or "clothe yourselves with"] the Lord Jesus Christ, and make no provision for the flesh, to gratify its desires.

Paul uses this image of shedding dirty clothes and putting on shining, clean armor to illustrate what it means spiritually to put off "dark deeds" and put on "right living" (NLT). Some of the dark deeds include wild parties and drunkenness, sexual sins, immoral living, arguing, and jealousy. But Paul does not instruct the church to simply *stop* participating in these activities; he also urges them to participate in, or "put on," alternative acts. These are activities that bring us into the presence of the Lord Jesus Christ.

In other words, Paul is saying, "Clothe yourself with Jesus." Similarly, Paul tells the Galatians this (3:27–28):

> As many of you as were baptized into Christ have clothed yourselves with Christ. There is no longer Jew or Greek, there is no longer slave or free, there is no longer male and female; for all of you are one in Christ Jesus.

Here, Paul connects "putting on new clothes" with baptism. This means that as the baptized people of God, we have been washed clean, removed of our dirty rags, and given a new, clean, fresh set of clothes. Our baptism has changed us: We have left the spirit of this world and received the Spirit of God.

As verse 28 indicates, through baptism, we have been incorporated into a new community that is *not* marked by ethnic, socioeconomic, or gender divisions but rather by oneness in Christ Jesus who has made us clean! We have been not only taken out of the swamp and brought into the castle but also completely transformed from our primitive existence and made a member of the royal family.

It's time to act and live accordingly. "As God's chosen ones, holy and beloved, *clothe yourselves* with compassion, kindness, humility, meekness, and patience" (Colossians 3:12, emphasis mine).

When scripture says to "clothe yourselves" with something, that means you are not already wearing the proper clothes! Though Christ has washed us clean in baptism, we may have easily slipped into our dirty rags again. Now that doesn't mean we need to be washed again. No, we have already been washed and received a new wardrobe. We simply need to repent and put on the new clothes we were meant to wear.

Of course, these are spiritual clothes that Paul is speaking of. I could be wearing an actual new outfit today, and yet my soul could be in filthy tatters. The *Shrek* movies portray this concept in the opposite way, with ugly ogres who are capable of love and virtue and heroics. Appearances do not always reflect what's on the inside.

What are you wearing? Have you resorted to wearing your old, dirty rags? Or are you wearing the clean clothes of Christ?

Though Christ has washed us clean in baptism, we may have easily slipped into our dirty rags again.

The improper clothing in Jesus's parable is in the context of a wedding. This setting is important.

If we know our Bible, we can't help but think about what Leithart calls the "fine beautiful clothing worn by the bride of Christ [the Church] at the wedding feast of the Lamb at the end of the book of Revelation," which is described as the "righteous acts of the saints." " 'To her it has been granted to be clothed with fine linen, bright and pure'— for the fine linen is the righteous deeds of the saints" (Revelation 19:8).

This bride of Christ in Revelation symbolizes the Church. And the Lamb—the groom—symbolizes Christ. In Revelation, we are a given this picture of a holy wedding between Christ and His Church. This is what God has always desired: to be in union—to be one—with His people. This is salvation—not simply to be saved *from* something but also to be saved *for* something—union with Christ.

Interestingly, both Revelation 19 and Matthew 22 describe weddings and both mention clothes. But in these two passages, clothing is not just clothing; it refers to the individual's inner being. The bride's dress, which is "fine linen, bright and clean," stands for a pure inner nature.

You may ask how we can say that about the Church. We know churches aren't perfect or pure. But the bride is not wearing righteousness because of her own efforts. We are told that the bride received the clothing of righteousness from her groom—Jesus Christ—and then put it on.

You see, in salvation, God's righteousness is given to us as a gift. But like any gift, we must cooperate with the giver in receiving it and putting it on. Knowing this helps us understand what is going on in Jesus's parable.

This is salvation—not simply to be saved *from* something but also to be saved *for* something— union with Christ.

In Matthew 22, a man attends the wedding feast that he is invited to; but he fails to cooperate with the host by not wearing the right clothes. This man who is thrown out of the wedding feast for his improper attire is meant to represent the religious who think they have a seat at the table because they have dressed themselves with religious activity. They look the part. They appear to have clean souls because they look good on the outside.

But when the King comes, He sees right through the costumes to the clothing of their hearts.

This is how we know that the man who is thrown out does not symbolize a poor beggar who cannot afford to dress properly for a wedding. Rather, the man being thrown out stands for the religious leaders who wear the finest religious garments, all while clothing their insides with arrogance and hatred.

By telling this parable, Jesus is issuing a strong warning to the religious leaders . . . and to us: at the day of judgment, when the King returns, He will judge us based on the way we dress.

You know how the day after a fancy awards ceremony, with celebrities and red carpets, the media points out the gowns and suits, evaluating which ones were triumphs and which were failures? Well, Jesus will do something similar, except that He looks past the appearances and straight to the heart. He will determine whether we are clothed in righteousness or whether we have dressed ourselves in worldly behaviors, or "dark deeds."

The good news for us is that the robes of righteousness are free! They are given to each of us in baptism. But we must choose to cooperate with Him by putting them on. We cannot simply leave them in our closets; we must wear them.

Have you ever heard the term "wedding crashing"? To crash a wedding is to attend a wedding celebration without an invitation. And yes, people do crash weddings, apparently for all different reasons. Some come for free catered food and alcoholic beverages, some to steal money or gifts for the bride and groom, and others to try to stop a wedding from happening or win back a former lover who is marrying someone else. There is even a movie called *Wedding Crashers*. In it, two guys crash weddings to pick up single women.

What do all these reasons have in common? They are all self-centered! I don't have to tell you that wedding crashing is not a good thing to do. And yet, I wonder if in our spiritual lives, we do something similar for selfish reasons.

This parable would have us ask ourselves these kinds of questions: *When we come to the wedding banquet of God, are we coming to celebrate Christ? Or are we coming for the food, beverages, entertainment, or whatever else the wedding has to offer? Do we come to the house of God thinking, "What can the church do for me?"—"What can God do for me?"—rather than seeing ourselves as unworthy guests lucky enough to be invited?*

In this parable, the application is clear. Jesus has invited many in. Not everyone accepts the invitation, and some are even hostile to it. But others do come.

Some who come do not belong, and that is obvious. They noticeably do not fit in because they come for the wrong reasons—and it shows. (Interestingly, those who do fit in are oftentimes the very same who do not fit into our society. This is the kind of beautiful, backwards, upside-downness of the kingdom.)

When we look at our own lives, what is our motivation for receiving Christ's call? Have we fooled ourselves into thinking we can follow Christ yet continue to live in sin?

Eugene Peterson paraphrases the Apostle Paul in Romans 6:1–3 (MSG) this way:

> So what do we do? Keep on sinning so God can keep on forgiving? I should hope not! If we've left the country where sin is sovereign, how can we still live in our old house there? Or didn't you realize we packed up and left there for good? That is what happened in baptism. When we went under the water, we left the old country of sin behind; when we came up out of the water, we entered into the new country of grace—a new life in a new land!

How can we continue to live as though we haven't been baptized into Jesus Christ? How can we continue to live in the old ways when the new has come?

If you are not an ogre—and I assume you're not—you probably would give up your shack in the swamp for a room in the palace in a heartbeat. When faced with the choice between the kingdom of God and these earthly digs—or worse, outer darkness—of course we would choose the kingdom. And yet despite that, the swamp seems to call to each one of us.

Wallowing in the mud of the swamp while being a member of the royal family is exactly what we're doing when we continue in sin after being baptized and proclaiming Jesus our Savior. It's showing up at the wedding feast in basketball shorts and a T-shirt.

I guess we have more in common with Shrek than we'd care to admit.

Are we simply showing up to witness the wedding, or are we here to participate? Are we showing up in the presence of the King wearing the dirty rags of the world when He has already gifted us with fine linen?

These are important questions to ask ourselves because *trust me*, the King knows the difference. Jesus makes that clear.

Each one of our lives is marked by an invitation. We have been invited into the King's courts. Jesus has called us off the streets to live in His Father's kingdom.

Some of us scorn the invitation. Some of us are even spiteful about it. Some of us come into the palace just to leave it and return to the streets. (Remember the Israelites in Exodus—they had left Egypt, but Egypt hadn't left them.)

And some of us sit comfortably in the palace, thinking we are safe because we have stayed in the banquet hall. We aren't going back to the streets. We may not be wearing the garb of wild parties, drunkenness, and drug use, but we have been comfortably outfitted in the garments of strife, pride, judgmentalism, and hatred. They have been our go-to outfits for years.

Jesus's warning is for those who are religious but not authentic in their faith. They are the ones who look good on the outside but are evil to God, who sees what's on the inside. We can all easily resort to this condition.

But there is a way out for all of us guests of the King. The gift of His forgiveness is also free with our new clothes. But just as we must choose to leave the streets, we must choose to wear our salvation, or the forgiveness is moot.

For Reflection or Discussion

1. In the Parable of the Wedding Banquet, the king's invitation is initially rejected by those who were originally invited. Reflect on your own life: How do you respond to God's invitations? Are there moments when you've ignored or rejected His call because it didn't align with your expectations or desires?

2. The king invites everyone, regardless of their status, to fill the wedding hall. How does this reflect on the inclusivity of God's kingdom? In what ways might you struggle with feeling "unworthy" of God's invitation, and how can this parable offer a new perspective on your value to God?

3. Reflect on the symbolic meaning of clothing in scripture. In what ways are you "clothing" yourself with Christ in your daily life? Are there areas where you might be neglecting to "put on" the character of Christ?

4. The king orders his servants to invite "everyone they find" to the wedding banquet. How does this reflect God's desire for a diverse kingdom? How can the Church better reflect this inclusivity in its community life?

5. The imagery of a wedding feast is a powerful picture of the joyous communion between Christ and His Church. How does anticipating this ultimate gathering with Christ shape your priorities and actions today? How does it influence your hope and outlook on the future?

THE STORIES THAT MAKE US

Wedding Clothes

THE STORIES THAT MAKE US

Wedding Clothes

The Parable of the Ten Bridesmaids

Matthew 25:1–13

Then the kingdom of heaven will be like this. Ten bridesmaids took their lamps and went to meet the bridegroom. Five of them were foolish, and five were wise. When the foolish took their lamps, they took no oil with them; but the wise took flasks of oil with their lamps. As the bridegroom was delayed, all of them became drowsy and slept. But at midnight there was a shout, "Look! Here is the bridegroom! Come out to meet him." Then all those bridesmaids got up and trimmed their lamps. The foolish said to the wise, "Give us some of your oil, for our lamps are going out." But the wise replied, "No! There will not be enough for you and for us; you had better go to the dealers and buy some for yourselves." And while they went to buy it, the bridegroom came, and those who were ready went in with him to the wedding banquet; and the door was shut. Later the other bridesmaids came also, saying, "Lord, lord, open to us." But he replied, "Truly I tell you, I do not know you." Keep awake therefore, for you know neither the day nor the hour.

THE STORIES THAT MAKE US

5

KEEPING WATCH

In the 1970s, a new music genre emerged called *punk rock*. The style is characterized by stripped-down instrumentation, fast-paced songs, and often, antiestablishment lyrics. Essentially, the genre was formed in and around youthful rebellion. At its peak, punk became a major cultural phenomenon, especially here in the United States and in the United Kingdom.

In the 1990s, the punk rock genre evolved and gave birth to other similar genres, such as alternative rock and pop punk.

When I was in high school, punk rock was popular. That being so, I listened to various punk, pop punk, and alternative rock artists, becoming quite familiar with the genre. One punk band called MxPx released a song titled "Responsibility," which features some of the youthful rebellion embedded within this genre of music. The chorus lyrics are telling:

> *Responsibility? What's that?*
> *... I don't want to think about it*
> *We'd be better off without it*

Despite what MxPx might say, the truth is that all of us, even if we do not want to, must come to terms with responsibility at *some point* in our lives. We cannot remain "punks"—or "worthless people," as the dictionary defines the word—forever. Even if we want to stay young and avoid accountability, at a certain age, we have to grow up and assume responsibility. And those who never do often live very difficult lives.

Even in the magical world of Peter Pan and Neverland, we understand that "All children, except one, grow up." Surely, only the foolish attempt to avoid adult responsibility forever, and they certainly are not as heroic and likable as Peter Pan, "the boy who wouldn't grow up."

And although punk rock lyrics may be quotable, they do not make for good life guidance. Now as a pastor, husband, and father, my relationship with punk rock has evolved. While I still appreciate the music, its themes of rebellion and avoiding responsibility resonate less with me. My roles have taught me the value of embracing responsibility, shaping a more mature perspective, and I assume most adults would feel the same.

Although many of us would laugh at or even scorn the unreasonable, immature attitude toward responsibility portrayed in the MxPx song, I bring these lyrics up because I want to suggest that—whether we realize it or not—we can all easily fall into such an attitude in our Christian lives. We may very well start to dodge our responsibilities as followers of Jesus Christ, joining the likes of the Lost Boys in an apathetic, but no less dangerous, spiritual Neverland.

And Jesus, knowing this—knowing our human condition—tells a story about ten virgins as a way to warn His disciples from falling into this common trap. In this story in Matthew 25, ten virgins take their lamps to meet the bridegroom. (Case-Winters explains that the original word here that is translated *virgins* is used generally to refer to any young, unmarried woman who is of a marriageable age. Rather than *virgin*, some translations use the word *bridesmaid*.)

Jesus is pulling from a first-century marriage custom whereby virgin bridesmaids would escort the bridegroom to the home of the bride. The bridesmaids would then accompany the couple to the house where the wedding celebration was to take place. Jesus takes this practice, with which His listeners would be familiar, and turns it into a story for their instruction.

In Jesus's story, ten virgins take their lamps to meet the bridegroom. We are told that five of the virgins are foolish and five are wise. The five *wise* ones take with them extra oil for their lamps; but the five who are *foolish* do not. In the story, the bridegroom is delayed, and the virgins understandably grow drowsy and fall asleep while waiting for him.

At midnight, they are awakened by a shout: "Look! Here is the bridegroom! Come out to meet him" (v. 6). The five wise virgins, who came prepared with extra oil, have enough to keep their lamps lit until the bridegroom appears; but they do not have enough to share with the five foolish virgins, whose lamps are lacking. The five foolish virgins, who did not bring extra oil for their lamps, must go to buy more because they have run out, and thus, they cannot see.

However, as Stanley Hauerwas says in his commentary on Matthew, "by the time the foolish virgins returned, the bridegroom had come, the wedding banquet had begun, and the door was shut." The virgins, having replenished their oil, then ask that the door be opened for them. But the bridegroom refuses, saying that he does not know them.

Then Jesus turns to His disciples and says, "Keep awake therefore, for you know neither the day nor the hour" (v. 13).

This is clearly a cautionary tale. But what does it mean? Furthermore, what is the parable trying to teach *us*? Why is Jesus contrasting the wise and the foolish? Or maybe a better question would be this: what does it mean to be foolish, and what does it mean to be wise?

Psalm 14:1 says, "Fools say in their hearts, 'There is no God.'" Basically, what makes one foolish is their rejection of God. As far as the wise are concerned, Proverbs 1:7 says, "The fear of the LORD is the beginning of knowledge." This wisdom is gained by following the Lord. Biblically then, what makes one foolish and what makes one wise is entirely dependent upon whether they hear and act upon God's word.

If we then asked Jesus our questions, perhaps He would say, "If you are wise, you will hear and follow My commandments. But if you are foolish, you won't and will suffer the consequences."

Yet we have to wonder why Jesus calls the five virgins who forgot to pack enough oil *foolish*. What is wrong with their going out to meet the bridegroom but simply forgetting to bring extra oil? We all forget things, don't we? Does that make us foolish or irresponsible? Or what if they assumed the bridegroom would be on time? I mean, I think that's a forgivable assumption to make!

Here is the key to this story: what made these virgins foolish is not how they *started* but rather how they *finished*. See, Jesus tells this parable to illustrate the need for all of us to be spiritually prepared while the Bridegroom—who is representative of Christ—is delayed in His return.

In the Bible, God's kingdom is compared to marriage. Ultimately, in the end, there will be a grand bringing-together, or a union—a marriage, if you will—between Christ and His bride, the Church. This is what God has always wanted—to be united with the image-bearers of His creation.

This story Jesus tells is about the future marriage of Christ and His Church at the end of the age. At this point, Christ—the Bridegroom—will return and bring the Church—His bride—into an eternal wedding banquet of celebration. This is what the parable is all about.

The problem is that some of the virgins—who represent all of humanity—are not prepared when the Bridegroom comes, or when Christ comes again. In His delay, people have fallen asleep.

This is what Jesus is essentially asking us: "Are you prepared for the Bridegroom to come? Have your lamps run out of oil? Have you fallen asleep while waiting?"

This is what God has always wanted—to be united with the image-bearers of His creation.

My wife, Anna, is a morning person. If you, like Anna, are also a morning person, I will refrain from judgment and simply say, you are both a mystery to me!

Because Anna is a morning person and I am not, we have two different philosophies for alarm-setting. I admittedly use and even *abuse* the snooze button. I do not like getting out of bed when the alarm sounds.

Unlike me, Anna will often just get up right after her alarm goes off. I usually hit the snooze button three or four times before I actually get up. But I would say I am not irresponsible or foolish because I plan for that. See, I set my alarm earlier than I need to get up because I know that I will hit snooze a few times. Makes perfect sense to me . . . but it drives Anna nuts.

But that is where the concept "love is patient" comes in, right? "For better or for worse" and all that? Thankfully, Anna does love me and puts up with my early morning snoozing despite it driving her crazy. And so I've got it good (and probably won't change my habit any time soon).

But one of the major downfalls of being a snooze-button addict are those times when I think I've hit the snooze button, and I've actually dismissed the alarm altogether and ended up sleeping later than I wanted to. Now, that has happened only a few times . . . but it *has* happened and once recently. This is a terrible feeling—waking up in a panic, realizing I have overslept.

Confession time: has this ever happened to you? If so, I can commiserate.

If we imagine this scene in Matthew 25, we can be sure that these young women experienced some panic when they realized that they had fallen asleep waiting on the bridegroom. In Jesus's parable, however, the bridegroom is delayed so long that all of the virgins drift off. They *all* fall asleep, and then, *all* are awakened by a loud, urgent alarm.

We might consider when Jesus's disciples fell asleep in the Garden of Gethsemane while waiting for Jesus, who was praying to His Father before He was arrested. In that case, Jesus scolded His disciples because they fell asleep while waiting. Yet in our parable, the fact that the ten virgins fall asleep does not seem to be a problem. They are not scolded for sleeping. In some ways, it seems understandable, considering the delay. Even the five wise virgins fall asleep.

This is because, in this parable, the virgins' sleep is a metaphor for death. There will be many who sleep (die) before the Bridegroom (Christ) comes to us, His bride (the Church). The simple fact of the matter is that in this world, the faithful (the wise) will die alongside the unfaithful (the foolish).

The virgins all being awakened at the cry at midnight is another metaphor. This alarm represents the time of Christ's Second Coming, when the wicked will arise with the righteous for judgment. When Christ comes again, *all* will rise—the faithful and the unfaithful.

In John 5:28–29, Jesus says this:

> Do not be astonished at this; for the hour is coming when all who are in their graves will hear his voice and will come out—those who have done good, to the resurrection of life, and those who have done evil, to the resurrection of condemnation.

Just like the parable, this teaching is to warn us that we must be prepared for Jesus's return, when all will be judged. Jesus also warns that He could come at any time: "Therefore, keep awake—for you do not know when the master of the house will come, in the evening, or at midnight, or at cockcrow, or at dawn" (Mark 13:35).

In Jesus's story, the foolish virgins are those who did not prepare for Christ's Second Coming. Of course, when the bridegroom comes, the five foolish virgins want the wise virgins to share their oil with them. But the five wise virgins tell them that they cannot. *Why?* Because it is impossible to enter God's new creation on account of someone else's faith. You cannot stand before God without your own faith or relationship with Jesus.

As such, the lamps and the oil represent the faith and good works of His disciples. Remember, Jesus says elsewhere that His disciples are to be the light of the world, like a lamp on a stand, and that they should let their good works shine before all people. So lacking light, or faith and good works, the foolish virgins are left in the dark. They believe the bridegroom is coming, but they do not prepare for his coming themselves.

This is the difference between the wise and the foolish: It's not that one believed that the bridegroom was coming and the others didn't. No! All of them believed he was coming. But only some of them allowed their belief—their expectation—to change the way they waited out the night.

The truth is that belief is not enough. Belief must take root and turn into living out that belief. James 2:19 says this: "You believe that God is one; you do well. Even the demons believe—and shudder."

> All of them believed [the bridegroom] was coming. But only some of them allowed their belief—their expectation—to change the way they waited out the night.

This parable lets us in on an important fact, which is that we need a continual supply of oil to keep our lamps lit. What distinguishes the wise from the foolish is that they allow their light to shine before others. Proverbs 13:9 says, "The light of the righteous rejoices, but the lamp of the wicked goes out."

Some of us may start out seeking the Bridegroom with true light, but if we do not persist, we can end up becoming foolish. If we do not continually refresh ourselves with new oil, our lights will not continue to burn. This is our responsibility—no one else can do this for us.

Another way of saying this is that some will hear Christ's words and begin to follow Him at first, but they will not continue. The worst part about this scenario is that they will be totally surprised by what happens as a result of their unpreparedness. They thought that merely believing in the Bridegroom was enough. But Jesus says it is not enough—only those who hear *and* obey are wise and allowed into the banquet.

So does this mean that faith in Jesus is not enough? Not exactly, because *true faith* is enough to get us through the waiting time. But true faith is a faith that produces true works. "So faith by itself, if it has no works, is dead" (James 2:17).

I have a theory I want to share with you. I think there are two types of people in the world: The first are those who see their car's gas warning light come on and go directly to the gas station (if they even wait for the light). And then there are the rest of us.

Perhaps we don't have enough excitement in our lives. So we test the waters, live on the side of danger, and see how long we can drive on an empty tank of gas. For me, it's a sort of game—a sick game that can potentially really ruin my day. But I play the game at least a few times a month. Not sure why, but I do.

But whether you are the type of person who fills up your tank as soon as the gas light comes on or not, my hunch is that most of us, at one time or another, have allowed our spiritual lives to run out of gas.

Like cars, the people of God need spiritual fuel—the energy to continue to allow our lights to burn before others. And this means that we need to be continually spiritually refueled.

In Jesus's parable, the five foolish virgins are prevented from entering the wedding feast because they run out of oil. And if we know our Bibles, we understand that throughout scripture, oil symbolizes the Spirit of God, who, as Leithart says, "energizes us to do good works." When deprived of the energy of the Spirit, the virgins in this parable "have no light to shine . . . [but] neither do we!"

Every single one of us needs a continual fresh supply of the Spirit to do what we are called to do. This is why our good works aren't really *our* good works—they are the result of God working in our lives as we yield to Him. This means that we must yield to the Spirit in our lives each and every day.

The ten virgins all started out yielding to the Spirit. Remember, at one time, they all had oil. But in the bridegroom's delay, they turned to other concerns. They all fell asleep. Some ran out of oil during the night.

Those believers who are out of oil may believe, but they certainly are not obeying. And in this sense, they are not *true* believers.

Jesus's warning should be heard by all of us: Be ready. Before we know it, we can become too comfortable in this world, living more for temporary pleasure and success, rather than living in hopeful expectation of Christ's coming.

I believe there is a reason, besides the cultural context, that this story casts virgins in the role of those who wait for the bridegroom. The virgins in this story represent the Church and Jesus's desire that the Church be presented to Him *purely*.

Paul says it this way in Ephesians 5:25–27:

> Christ loved the church and gave himself up for her, that he might sanctify her, having cleansed her by the washing of water with the word, so that he might present the church to himself in splendor, without spot or wrinkle or any such thing, that she might be holy and without blemish.

It is not as if our actions make us pure, holy, and blameless. No—Christ has already done that for us. But the message in this parable is that we must *choose* to accept what Christ has done for us and continue walking in the Spirit toward that glorious future He has gifted and prepared for us.

If you haven't fallen asleep, if you are still waiting in this world, then you have the opportunity right now to ask God whether you are living foolishly or wisely. If Christ shows up today, what would your reaction be?

Are you prepared? Have you been shining your light, or are you in the dark? Are you hearing and obeying the words of Christ, or have you bucked your responsibility to pursue your own desires—like Peter Pan, crowing the merits of your own cleverness? Are you keeping your lamp burning by allowing the Spirit of God to develop the fruit of the Spirit in your life? Or in His "delay," have you turned to other matters? Have you, weary of waiting, allowed your lamp to go out?

In Ephesians 5:18 (NIV), Paul says, "Don't be drunk with wine, because that will ruin your life. Instead, be filled with the Holy Spirit." Just like alcohol can control a person when they are intoxicated—how they walk, how they talk, how they live—so we, when we are filled with the Holy Spirit, walk, talk, and live differently. The Holy Spirit, in this way, is a divine intoxicant. This intoxicant, though, rather than wrecking your life, sets it on a firm foundation.

Being filled with the Spirit, which leads to living in the Spirit, keeps our lamps burning. Ask Him for a fresh supply of His oil to wait out the night.

For Reflection or Discussion

1. The foolish virgins were unprepared for the bridegroom's arrival. Can you identify areas in your life where you might be spiritually unprepared or complacent?

2. Consider the role of the Holy Spirit (symbolized by oil in many biblical passages) in your life. How regularly do you seek to be filled with the Spirit to sustain your spiritual light?

3. The wise virgins brought extra oil for their lamps. How does this action parallel maintaining a reliance upon the Spirit's "oil" in our lives during periods of waiting or uncertainty?

4. The parable ends with a sobering reminder that not all who wait are known by the bridegroom. How does this underscore the importance of a personal and authentic relationship with Christ?

5. The parable suggests that faith must be accompanied by actions that demonstrate readiness and wisdom. What spiritual practices/disciplines might God be calling you toward that help foster a faith that not only believes in Christ's return but actively prepares for it?

Keeping Watch

THE STORIES THAT MAKE US

Keeping Watch

The Parable of the Three Servants

Matthew 25:14–30

For it is as if a man, going on a journey, summoned his slaves and entrusted his property to them; to one he gave five talents, to another two, to another one, to each according to his ability. Then he went away. The one who had received the five talents went off at once and traded with them, and made five more talents. In the same way, the one who had the two talents made two more talents. But the one who had received the one talent went off and dug a hole in the ground and hid his master's money. After a long time the master of those slaves came and settled accounts with them. Then the one who had received the five talents came forward, bringing five more talents, saying, "Master, you handed over to me five talents; see, I have made five more talents." His master said to him, "Well done, good and trustworthy slave; you have been trustworthy in a few things, I will put you in charge of many things; enter into the joy of your master." And the one with the two talents also came forward, saying, "Master, you handed over to me two talents; see, I have made two more talents." His master said to him, "Well done, good and trustworthy slave; you have been trustworthy in a few things, I will put you in charge of many things; enter into the joy of your master." Then the one who had received the one talent also came forward, saying, "Master, I knew that you were a harsh man, reaping where you did not sow, and gathering where you did not scatter seed; so I was afraid, and I went and hid your talent in the ground. Here you have what is yours." But his master replied, "You wicked and lazy slave! You knew, did you, that I reap where I did not sow, and gather where I did not scatter? Then you ought to have invested my money with the bankers, and on my return I would have received what was my own with interest. So take the talent from him, and give it to the one with the ten talents. For to all those who have, more will be given, and they will have an abundance; but from those who have nothing, even what they have will be taken away. As for this worthless slave, throw him into the outer darkness, where there will be weeping and gnashing of teeth."

6

STEWARDING OUR VIEWS OF GOD

Robin Hood, the mythical heroic outlaw who gained prominence through literature and film, was originally an English legend. According to folklore, Robin was a skilled archer and swordsman who robbed the rich to give to the poor.

Through variations and retellings of this legend, the hooded outlaw in green acquired a supporting cast. In some versions of the story, Robin's arch nemesis, the Sheriff of Nottingham, assists the cruel and greedy Prince John in seizing King Richard's throne while the king is away fighting battles. In this telling, Robin is loyal to King Richard and thus opposes Prince John's takeover.

Even though the original legend of Robin Hood was not set during the reign of King Richard I, this is perhaps the most popular version of the story today. Historically, King Richard I ruled England from 1189 to 1199. Most of his reign was spent abroad, fighting in the Crusades, and he was even captured at one point. His brother, Prince John, gained support in the king's absence to take the English throne. However, when

King Richard eventually returned home, he took back the throne as the rightful ruler of England.

It's got all the elements of a caper. First, we've got a well-intentioned hero/criminal who takes it upon himself to redistribute the country's wealth—by stealing. Second is the sheriff, who in medieval England would have not only been the local law enforcer but also the collector of debts. Third is the power-hungry prince. And all of their shenanigans are possible because the king is AWOL.

The story of Robin Hood, with its emphasis on the mismanagement of money and its setting within the historical event of an absent king, resonates with Jesus's parable of the talents.

In Matthew 25:14–30, Jesus tells about a man who, before going away for a long time, divided his money among his servants to be managed. After the man returns, he asks his servants to give an account of how they had used the money. The servant who had received five bags of silver invested it and gained five more. For him, his master is full of praise. The second servant had been given two bags of silver; he also invested it and generated two more. The master celebrates this servant's accomplishment as well.

However, the last servant, who had been given one bag of silver, buried it in the ground because he was afraid. The master scolds the servant and calls him "wicked and lazy" (v. 26). As a result, the money is taken from him and given to the servant with the ten bags of silver.

Jesus ends the tale by saying, "For to all those who have, more will be given, and they will have an abundance; but from those who have nothing, even what they have will be taken away" (v. 29).

The main theme of this parable is stewardship. Stewardship involves responsible planning and proper management of resources. Now, we can find the concept of stewardship in the story Robin Hood, but it is not the responsible, proper kind. Robin may have seen himself as the ultimate steward, and although his intentions may have been charitable, I somehow don't think Jesus would approve of his methods.

Jesus's story has to do with wise investment. The issue is not how much is given to each servant to invest; the one with the five bags and the one with the two bags receive the same amount of praise. And so the emphasis is not on how much the servants received but on how the servants *stewarded* what they received.

If we were to craft a moral for the parable, it would be that those who invest and increase what God has given them will be given more; but those who bury and waste what they have received will lose even that which they have been given.

Perhaps this is what Robin Hood was attempting to do by taking away the wealth that the nobles had stored up for themselves. It only makes sense that we can be more generous when we have more to give. This is how the king is able to give more to those servants who had created more wealth for him.

It comes down to this: we must use what God has given us for His service.

We see this theme throughout scripture. Moses and David—perhaps the two most popular characters in the Old Testament—began as humble shepherds. Because of their faithfulness in the small and menial, they are raised up by God.

When God calls Moses to deliver His people from slavery in Egypt, Moses can only see what he is lacking. He doesn't think he is a good enough speaker, and he frankly tells God this! Unlike Prince John, who was conspiring to seize power he didn't deserve, Moses declares he is unworthy to be the deliverer of God's people. But God chooses Moses not because of his skill, but because Moses is faithful in the little things.

David—considered the greatest king in all of Israel's history—was at first overlooked. God tells the prophet Samuel that He is calling someone within Jesse's family to be the next king of Israel. And so, Jesse rounds up his strapping boys for Samuel to meet and choose from. But Samuel knows that the future king, whom God has called, is not among them.

Samuel then asks Jesse if he has any other sons. Jesse tells Samuel about his youngest, David, who is watching over the sheep. When he meets the boy David, Samuel knows he is looking at the future king of Israel.

Because of their faithfulness in the small and menial, Moses and David are elevated—promoted from watching over flocks of sheep to caring for God's sheep, the people of Israel.

The truth is that we may feel lack in our lives; we may think we have nothing to offer God and others. But when we are faithful with the little that we do have, God elevates our capacity in service so that we can better love Him and love others well.

If you have ever heard this parable taught before, you were probably told that it is about the stewardship of spiritual gifts—that we need to put what God has given us "to work." And it's true: God has given us each abilities, money, and time. If we are hoarding those gifts, keeping them to ourselves, and not investing them into God's kingdom, then we are like the wicked and lazy servant who buried what he was given.

In this way, we are to follow the wisdom in Proverbs 3:9 (NLT): "Honor the LORD with your wealth and with the best part of everything you produce." Whatever it is that God has given us, we must put it to use for God's glory.

But Leithart tells us that in another sense, the treasure Jesus is talking about is the "treasure that He gives His church, the treasure of the gospel" and the part we have to play "in proclaiming, elaborating, and applying that gospel."

We have all received the gospel and ministry through Jesus, who has cleansed us from our sin, has set us into right relationship with God, and is changing us from the inside out through the power of the Holy Spirit. But the question then becomes this: how are we applying what we have received?

Are we like the servant who hoards this gift by burying it? Like the affluent in Robin Hood's day who kept the riches for themselves while the less fortunate suffered and starved? Or are we applying our gifts by sharing our faith, living righteous lives, giving to the ministry of the church, giving to the poor and needy, and showing mercy and love to the stranger?

We each have received a rich gift of grace and must begin to invest it into the world. But along with stewardship is another important facet to this story that does not get as much attention.

Brad Young, in his book *The Parables*, lets us know that like the rest of Jesus's parables, the setting for this one is taken from the everyday lives of people in Jesus's time on Earth. During this time, entrusting money to servants was not an unusual scenario. Servants were sometimes entrusted with money and were expected to be responsible for it and to exercise wise judgment over it.

The reason that the last servant was rebuked was because he was not wise—he was not responsible in his care of the silver. As the text says, the servant was afraid. Fear—not wisdom—dictated his actions.

Perhaps one of the greatest baseball films ever made is *The Sandlot*. This 1993 film, set in the 1960s, follows a group of boys who play baseball every day in a local sandlot. A nerdy, reserved fifth grader, Scotty Smalls, moves with his mother and stepfather to this new town, where he has difficulty making friends until he is invited to play baseball with the boys. This would be great, except that Scotty is unable to throw or catch a baseball. Eventually, with help from one of the players, named Benny, Scotty learns the basics and becomes one of "the guys."

Then one day, Benny hits the team's last baseball so hard that it knocks the cover off. While his stepfather is on a business trip, Scotty decides to borrow an autographed baseball from home, not realizing that Babe Ruth's signature makes this baseball unlike any other. With it, Scotty hits his first home run, over the fence and into a yard where a giant dog, nicknamed "The Beast," is tied up.

The boys are terrified. They believe the legend that says the Beast is a giant gorilla-dog that once ate a human. According to the legend, the owner, Mr. Mertle, had to confine the dog in his backyard forever after the incident. The legend also has that Mr. Mertle is a mean old man.

When the other boys learn about the autograph, they make several attempts to rescue the ball from the yard using makeshift retrieval devices. But each is ultimately destroyed by the Beast.

After their efforts to retrieve the baseball fail, they eventually meet Mr. Mertle and find out that he and the dog, whose real name is Hercules, are quite kind. Mr. Mertle had once played baseball with Babe Ruth but was struck blind by an errant pitch. He replaces the ball that the dog chewed with one autographed by Ruth and all of the 1927 Yankees players, which Scotty gives to his stepdad. The boys resume playing in the sandlot, with Hercules, their new mascot.

This kids' classic surprised adult audiences when it was released with its charm and wholesomeness. But its nostalgia is even more powerful today, making it one of the most popular baseball movies, holding its own with such greats as *Field of Dreams* and *A League of Their Own*.

For us, seeking to understand the Parable of the Three Servants, the valuable parts of this movie are its depictions of the boys' efforts to extract the baseball from the backyard where the Beast lives. Because the boys believe something false about the dog—that he is vicious and once ate a human—they respond accordingly. They live in fear of the dog and its owner, thus restricting their success in rescuing the rare, autographed baseball.

But as the boys find out, the legend is bogus. Because they believed something untrue about the dog and its owner, the kids were unable to accomplish their mission.

In the same way, in Jesus's story, the servant who buried his silver did so because he believed something false about his master. Let's look at what he said once again in Matthew 25:24–26:

> Then the one who had received the one talent also came forward, saying, "Master, I knew that you were a harsh man, reaping where you did not sow, and gathering where you did not scatter seed; so I was afraid, and I went and hid your talent in the ground. Here you have what is yours."

Because of his fear of his master, the servant was frozen, incompetent, incapable of investing what he had been given. Put another way, because the servant had a faulty view of his master, he lived in a way that squelched his true potential.

The same is true for us; when we live with a distorted view of God, we will live in distorted, unwise ways—ways that are in fact harmful to us. See, stewardship and theology are intimately related: what we think about God will influence how we live our lives.

Emil Brunner said, "There is only one question which is really serious, and that is the question concerning the being and nature of God. From this all other questions derive their significance."

> Stewardship and theology are intimately related: what we think about God will influence how we live our lives.

The master of the parable is thought to be a harsh man. But he isn't that kind of master. Leithart tells us that the servant failed to see that he served a generous master, who gave him a valuable gift and desired to reward him for faithfulness. But because of his misconceptions of his master, the servant lived unfaithfully.

His master wasn't controlling; he was forbearing. The master trusted his servants. But the third servant did not seem to know the master *at all*.

This parable begs us to reflect on our own views of our Master. Theologian Clark Pinnock says this about it:

They weren't not told how to invest it, whether in a train of camels or in the grain trade. They are free to invest it however they choose. The one thing required is that they not be afraid to take chances and they not be afraid of their master.... [In the same way, it] is faith in the Father's love that frees us to take risk[s].

If we only fear God, we will not live life to the fullest, in which we experience the good, beautiful, and true life that God has offered us. He has released us with the gift of His gospel to live in His kingdom. He has released us to take risks for His kingdom.

In this parable, two of the servants feared and loved the master, and the third only feared him. In our Christian faith, there is a healthy fear—an amazement or a wonderment—of God. At the same time, God invites us to love Him *and* to be loved by Him.

Jesus says that His disciples should not consider themselves servants or slaves but instead friends of Christ (John 15:15). Do you know this about yourself? That you are a friend of Jesus? Teresa of Avila said, "We shall never be able to know ourselves, except we endeavor to know God."

We do not have to come to God trembling in fear but in utter confidence because of what Christ has done for us. He has destroyed death and welcomed us in. As John says, "God is love" (1 John 4:8).

But A. W. Tozer is right: "What comes into our minds when we think about God is the most important thing about us."

If we, like the third servant, think God is harsh and unapproachable, we will not live free. We will be timid to apply the gospel to our lives and wary to share the Good News because, deep down, we don't believe it to be *good* news. We might think to ourselves, "Maybe it is true—but surely it isn't good." We, of course, would be completely mistaken. When we view God aright, we recognize that He is pure goodness and love.

In a course that my church offered for facilitating emotionally healthy relationships, the participants learned a relational skill that would help us stop trying to read others' minds and instead clarify expectations. Our class discovered that whether we realize it or not, all of us assume we know what people are thinking and feeling all the time. In this way, we trick ourselves into believing we can mind-read!

We tell ourselves stories about others based on their actions (or our interpretations of their actions) that simply are not true. We make assumptions without checking them out, which damages friendships, families, and relationships in churches and workplaces. For instance, you know when you text someone and they never text you back? Don't we assume they are mad or annoyed at us? We may even decide that they are being childish or insensitive or rude for not replying. We end up assuming things about people that are not true.

And we do the same to God, as this parable points out.

Imagine with me for a moment what is going on in the servant's head. I wonder if the servant's flawed understanding of his master was influenced by his master's *absence*. I suggest this possibility because often our own perception of God's goodness and love is influenced by what feels like His absence.

When we go through something difficult, and we don't sense God's presence with us, we assume things about God. Either "He doesn't care," or "He's punishing me," or "He likes *them* better," and so on and so on.

Perhaps some of us have felt like God was absent when He should have been present with us. We interpret that to be abandonment, and thus, we live life as though we serve a God who has left us for good. Like the servant, we live fearful and in a state of neglect rather than joyful and in a state of adoption.

The truth is that God's presence does not come and go. God has promised to never leave His people (Joshua 1:9) and to be with them always (Matthew 28:20). Yet at times, it may seem like He has truly departed. For times such as these, we must know that our sense of God can be unreliable. We may feel as if He has left us, but in fact, He has been closer to us than we can even discern.

It is like when Jesus heals the man who had born blind in John 9. Jesus heals the blind man by anointing his eyes with mud and then instructing him to wash in a pool. Once the man's eyes are open, Jesus is gone. Then the man is left to engage in a back-and-forth with the Pharisees, who interrogate him about his healing. And because this man is not yet a follower of Jesus, he does not have adequate answers to their questions.

In some ways, it might seem that Jesus abandoned this man at the worst possible time. Yet we find out that He never really left. At the end of the interrogation, Jesus appears again, revealing Himself to the once-blind man in a deeper way than He had before.

Like the servant, we live fearful and in a state of neglect rather than joyful and in a state of adoption.

The truth is this: God doesn't leave us. He doesn't forsake us. But we may experience feelings of abandonment. It is what we choose to do in His perceived absence that makes all the difference—as we are taught in this parable. For this reason, says Chris E. W. Green in *Surprised by God*, we must ask ourselves: *how am I practicing the absence of God?*

Like the third servant, are we merely burying the gift of the gospel? Are we choosing to believe a lie about God's character because of a perception of distance? Or in His "absence," will we choose to discover Him afresh?

Henri Nouwen in *Reaching Out* puts it this way:

> The spiritual life is, first of all, a patient waiting.... It is in the center of our ... longing for the absent God that we discover his footprints.... Just as the love of a mother for her son can grow deeper when he is far away, just as children can learn to appreciate their parents more when they leave the home, just as lovers can rediscover each other during long periods of absence, so our intimate relationship with God can become deeper and more mature by the purifying experience of his absence.

This parable alerts us to the need to pay attention to what we do in God's perceived absence. How are you awaiting your Master's return?

For Reflection or Discussion

1. Fear played a significant role in the decisions made by the servant who buried his talent. How does fear influence your decisions, especially regarding the use of the gifts and resources you've been given?

2. Considering the biblical figures of Moses and David, who were elevated due to their faithfulness in seemingly small tasks, how do you value and approach the small responsibilities entrusted to you? Do you see them as opportunities for growth and service, or do you tend to overlook their importance?

3. Considering the interconnectedness of stewardship and theology, how do your beliefs about God shape your understanding and practice of stewardship? Are you living in a way that reflects a trust in God's goodness and generosity, or are you allowing fear and misunderstanding to dictate your actions?

4. The misinterpretation of the master's character by the third servant led to inaction and loss. How do you ensure your understanding of God's character is accurate and rooted in scripture, and how does this understanding influence your daily decisions and actions?

5. How do you navigate the periods in your life when you feel God's presence is missing, similar to the servant's flawed perception of his master's character and intentions? In these moments of perceived absence, how do you maintain or rebuild your faith and trust in God's constant presence and goodness, even when it feels like He is far away?

THE STORIES THAT MAKE US

Stewarding Our Views of God

THE STORIES THAT MAKE US

Stewarding Our Views of God

THE STORIES THAT MAKE US

POSTSCRIPT

If I may offer a concluding thought, it is this: The journey of engaging with Jesus's parables is not merely a religious exercise but a profound spiritual encounter that invites us to live differently. As we close this book, let's remember that the teachings of Jesus are meant to be lived out, not just pondered in isolation. They call us to action, to a transformation that goes beyond our individual experiences and extends to our communities and the wider world.

Throughout this book, we've explored how Jesus's parables challenge our perceptions and prompt us to reconsider our priorities. As you reflect on these stories, consider how they might reshape your approach to daily living. Are there areas in your life where Jesus's teachings have yet to re-story your life? What changes might you make to align more closely with the truths that Jesus lays out?

My prayer is that this book has not only deepened your understanding but also sparked a desire to live more intentionally in Christ's love, compassion, and justice. May you find in the teachings of Jesus a path that leads to a fuller, more purposeful life.

Thank you for accompanying me on this journey. May the parables of Jesus continue to challenge and move you toward greater intimacy with Christ.

WORKS CITED

Barth, Karl. *Church Dogmatics: The Doctrine of Reconciliation*, Vol. 4, pt. 1. London: T&T Clark International, 2004.

Case-Winters, Anna. *Matthew: A Theological Commentary on the Bible*. Louisville, KY: Westminster John Knox Press, 2015.

Chafer, Lewis Sperry, and John F. Walvoord. *Major Bible Themes: 52 Vital Doctrines of the Scriptures Simplified and Explained*. Grand Rapids, MI: Zondervan, 1974.

Green, Chris E. W. *Surprised by God: How and Why What We Think about God Matters*. Eugene, OR: Cascade Books, 2018.

Hauerwas, Stanley. *Matthew*. Grand Rapids, MI: Brazos Press, 2006.

"History of the High Sheriff." Lord-Lieutenant of Cornwall. https://lordlieutenantofcornwall.org.uk/history-of-the-high-sheriff/.

Leithart, Peter J. *The Gospel of Matthew through New Eyes: Jesus as Israel*. 2 vols. West Monroe, LA: Athanasius Press, 2019.

Nouwen, Henri J. M. *Reaching Out: The Three Movements of the Spiritual Life*. New York: Doubleday, 1975.

Pagola, José A. *The Way Opened Up by Jesus: A Commentary on the Gospel of Matthew*. Miami, FL: Convivium Press, 2012.

Pangambam, S. "The Clues to a Great Story by Andrew Stanton at TED (Full Transcript)." March 21, 2016. https://singjupost.com/the-clues-to-a-great-story-by-andrew-stanton-at-ted-full-transcript/.

Pennington, Jonathan T. *The Sermon on the Mount and Human Flourishing: A Theological Commentary*. Grand Rapids, MI: Baker

Academic, 2017.

"Pilot Dies and Passenger, 81, Lands Cessna." *Los Angeles Times*, June 18, 1998. https://www.latimes.com/archives/la-xpm-1998-jun-18-mn-61237-story.html.

Pinnock, Clark H., and Robert C. Brow. *Unbounded Love: A Good News Theology for the 21st Century*. Eugene, OR: Wipf and Stock Publishers, 2000.

Pippert, Rebecca Manley. *Hope Has Its Reasons: The Search to Satisfy Our Deepest Longings*. Downers Grove, IL: InterVarsity, 2001.

"Responsibility," track 3 on MxPx, *The Ever Passing Moment*, A&M Records, 2000.

Ritzema, Elliot, ed. *300 Quotations for Preachers*. Bellingham, WA: Lexham Press, 2012.

"Sermon Illustrations." PreachingToday.com. https://www.preachingtoday.com/illustrations/.

"Seven." In *Zondervan Dictionary of Biblical Imagery*, edited by John A. Beck, 774–75. Grand Rapids, MI: Zondervan, 2011.

Smith, James Bryan. *Hidden in Christ: Living as God's Beloved*. Downers Grove, IL: IVP Books, 2013.

Tozer, A. W. *The Knowledge of the Holy*. London: James Clarke & Co., 1965.

Volf, Miroslav. *Exclusion and Embrace: A Theological Exploration of Identity, Otherness, and Reconciliation*. Nashville, TN: Abingdon Press, 1996.

Weinstein, Miriam. *The Surprising Power of Family Meals: How Eating Together Makes Us Smarter, Stronger, Healthier, and Happier*. Lebanon, NH: Steerforth Press, 2005.

Wesley, John. *Forty-Four Sermons*. London: The Epworth Press, 1965.

Willard, Dallas. *The Divine Conspiracy: Rediscovering Our Hidden Life in God*. New York: HarperCollins Publishers, 1998.

Young, Brad H. *The Parables: Jewish Tradition and Christian Interpretation*. Peabody: MA, Hendrickson Publishers, 1998.

Andrew Ray Williams (PhD, Bangor University, United Kingdom) is the lead pastor at Church on the Hill in Fishersville, Virginia, and an adjunct professor at Life Pacific University. He is honored to be a St. Basil Fellow at the Center for Pastor Theologians and a member of the International Lutheran-Pentecostal Ecumenical Dialogue. Andrew is the author of multiple books, including *Reconstructing Prayer* (2023), *Washed in the Spirit* (2021), and *Boundless Love* (2021), and a co-editor with Patrick Oden of *Theological Renewal for the Third Millennium* (2022). His first poetry collection, *A Funeral in the Wild*, was published in 2024. He and his wife, Anna, have three children: Adelaide, Audrey, and Anderson.

Made in the USA
Middletown, DE
21 February 2025

71521186R00077